To give praise, honor,
and glory to God,
this book is dedicated to

The Father,

The Son,

and

The Holy Spirit.

A DIVINE REVELATION of the Spirit Realm

A DIVINE REVELATION OF THE Spirit Realm

MARY K. BAXTER

Whitaker House

A DIVINE REVELATION OF THE SPIRIT REALM

For speaking engagements, please contact:
Lowery Ministries International
P.O. Box 2550
Cleveland, TN 37320-2550

ISBN: 0-88368-623-6
Printed in the United States of America
© 2000 by Lowery Ministries International

Whitaker House
30 Hunt Valley Circle
New Kensington, PA 15068

Library of Congress Cataloging-in-Publication Data

Baxter, Mary K.
  A divine revelation of the spirit realm / Mary K. Baxter
  with T.L. Lowery.
       p. cm.
  ISBN 0-88368-623-6 (pbk.: alk. paper)
    1. Spiritual warfare.   2. Private revelations.   3. Visions.
    4. Baxter, Mary K.   I. Lowery, T. L. (Thomas Lanier), 1929–
  II. Title.
BV4509.5 .B394 2001
291.4'2—dc21   00-012627

CONTENTS

Foreword

Mary Kathryn Baxter is a choice servant of the Lord. She lives close to God, and He rewards her faithfulness by giving her special revelations. As she makes it clear in this book, God tells her to share the things He shows her with the people of the world. This she does by speaking in churches and conferences all around the world and through her writings.

Mary Baxter's two previous national best-selling books, *A Divine Revelation of Hell* and *A Divine Revelation of Heaven,* are being read and enjoyed by a vast reading public. They have been published in many different countries and in many languages. Millions of people around the world have read them and have been blessed. She has received reports of many who have repented and turned to Christ through their message.

I believe that this book will experience the same spectacular success and that many more people will find the Lord through reading it.

As Mary Baxter's pastor for several years, I have first-hand knowledge of her love for God and the way that He has, in turn, placed His approval on her work. The anointing of God upon her life gives what she does a wide acceptance.

Much prayer, hard work, and diligence have gone into the processing of this book. I pray that its wide distribution will bring many souls into the kingdom of God and will bring honor to the name of the One whom we love and adore.

—*T. L. Lowery, Ph.D.*

Introduction

Following the same pattern I set in my two previous books, *A Divine Revelation of Hell* and *A Divine Revelation of Heaven*, I am relating a series of visions and revelations of the spirit world that God showed to me at special times in my life.

My blessed Lord allowed me to see both good and bad spirits—angels and demons—and He showed me how the vast empire of Satan operates. Spiritual warfare is a continuing reality, a battle that is being waged every day. My heart goes out to all who are lost and especially to those who are bound in any way by evil spirits.

In these special revelations God told me that believers can gain victory in their spiritual battles if they will only follow His Word. I have found that obedience brings results every time!

It is the sincere desire of my heart to help equip other believers with the knowledge of what the Bible says about the way that Satan operates. I want them to know that we can gain victory over the devil and all his forces every day. My prayer is that as you read these pages, your faith will grow stronger in Jesus!

I want to give special honor and thanks to Pastor T. L. Lowery and to his beautiful wife, Mildred, for their support and encouragement in the writing of this book. Without them, it would not have been written.

Also, I want to thank Reverend Marcus V. Hand for his editorial guidance in this project. I gratefully acknowledge, recognize, and credit the staff at Whitaker House in New Kensington, Pennsylvania, who have been instrumental in making all of my works available to the reading public.

Above all, and with a grateful heart, I thank Jesus, who has called me to share this message.

And I thank you, the reader, for prayerfully reading these words and for allowing Him to apply them to your hearts. May God bless you all!

—Mary K. Baxter

To Kathryn from Jesus

For this purpose you were born,
to write and tell
what I have shown and told you,
for these things are faithful and true.
Your call is to let the world know
that there is a heaven,
that there is a hell,
and that I, Jesus, was sent by the Father
to save them from torment
and to prepare a place for them
in heaven.

Chapter 1

My Revelation of the Spirit Realm

In my previous books I have told of God's special revelations to me. In the first series of my revelatory experiences, Jesus led me into hell and showed me the indescribable and unimaginable horrors that await those who go to that awful place of doomed souls. I tried to tell others what I was seeing, and at first they would not believe me.

But God told me, "I am going to reveal to you the reality of hell. I will show you these things so that many may be saved and many can repent of their evil ways before it is too late."

He continued solemnly, "Your soul will be taken out of your body by Me, the

Lord Jesus Christ. You will be conveyed supernaturally into hell and to other places in the spirit realm. You will be able to see things that you cannot see in the natural realm, but these are the things I want you to see."

Since then, my blessed Lord has so graciously allowed me to put the things that He showed me into print. These books have been read by millions of people in many countries around the world.

WHY GOD GIVES REVELATIONS

From the countless reports I have received, multitudes have been saved as a result of reading about the things God showed me. Oh, the pain and tortures that await those who have not been born again! What judgment awaits those who don't know the Lord Jesus Christ!

God also spoke to me and said, "I will also show you visions of heaven and other places, and give you many revelations." I have described my visits to heaven in another book.

Thank God, He is using this account of my experiences in a marvelous way.

Again, my soul was seemingly lifted from my body and conveyed to a beautiful, marvelous, glorious realm.

Friends, I want to tell you that heaven is real, just as hell is real. If you do not know Jesus as your Savior and Lord, I urge you to repent and be saved, for the kingdom of God is at hand.

I am an ordinary person, but one whom God has touched in a supernatural way. He has given me a special message and commissioned me to tell it as well as publish it. I am obeying Him.

In my visions I have been permitted to see millions of angels and demons. I saw them engaged in many different tasks. The angels I saw in heaven were always and constantly praising and glorifying God.

Jesus reassured me by showing how the Bible confirms what I saw:

> [11] And I beheld, and I heard the voice of many angels round about the throne and the beasts and the elders: and the number of them was ten thousand times ten thousand, and thousands of thousands.

¹² Saying with a loud voice, Worthy is the Lamb that was slain to receive power, and riches, and wisdom, and strength, and honour, and glory, and blessing.

¹³ And every creature which is in heaven, and on the earth, and under the earth, and such as are in the sea, and all that are in them, heard I saying, Blessing, and honour, and glory, and power, be unto him that sitteth upon the throne, and unto the Lamb for ever and ever.

¹⁴ And the four beasts said, Amen. And the four and twenty elders fell down and worshipped him that liveth for ever and ever.

(Revelation 5:11–14)

Angels are more than a gimmick for a television sitcom. They are real spirit beings, created by God, who are sometimes visible and sometimes invisible.

They travel freely back and forth between earth and heaven, just as Jacob saw in his vision of the golden ladder:

¹² And he dreamed, and behold a ladder set up on the earth, and the

top of it reached to heaven: and behold the angels of God ascending and descending on it.

(Genesis 28:12)

In Mark 8:38 Jesus called them *"holy angels,"* so we know God created them holy.

ANGEL ALLIES

In my tour of the spiritual realm, I came to see that each angel of God has distinct responsibilities and duties. Afterward I remembered that the Bible gives a glimpse of the organization of holy angels in Colossians:

> [16] For by him were all things created, that are in heaven, and that are in earth, visible and invisible, whether they be thrones, or dominions, or principalities, or powers: all things were created by him, and for him.   (Colossians 1:16)

The angelic realm includes holy beings called seraphim, cherubim, archangels, and angels, as well as thrones, dominions, principalities, and powers.

Many interesting facts about angels are given in the Bible:

- 📖 Angels are beautiful specimens of God's creative grace who sing to mortals, just as they did to the shepherds when Jesus was born (Luke 2:13–14).
- 📖 Angels are divine messengers, or couriers, from God who bring special messages to His people, just as they did to Abraham in Genesis 18 and to Joseph in Matthew 1:20–21.
- 📖 Angels are messengers of doom who sometimes execute God's judgment on the disobedient, just as they did on Jerusalem in 2 Samuel 24:15–16.
- 📖 Angels are fierce warriors who oppose demons (see Daniel 10:13, 21) and fight real battles with them (see Jude 9).
- 📖 Angels are compassionate beings who watch over children, just as Jesus talked about in Matthew 18:10.
- 📖 Angels are described in Hebrews 1:14 as *"ministering spirits."*

THE EVIL OPPOSITION

However, there is a dark, sinister side to the unseen spirit world around us. Just as God is real, so Satan, the evil one, is real.

Just as God has an unnumbered multitude of angels to carry out His works and His plans, so Satan has an unnumbered host of evil spirits. They go about at his bidding, and they work hard all the time to carry out the wishes of the prince of demons.

The angels are greater in number than the evil spirits, but the spirits of darkness I saw were all working feverishly. I wondered about all their activity.

"Why are they all working so hard?" I asked Jesus.

He satisfied my curiosity with a profound, yet simple, answer: "Because they all know that their time is short and their fate is doomed. They know they will be lost eternally, and they want to deceive as many as they can and take them with them."

God showed me this spirit world. He opened up and revealed to me the inner workings of the whole empire of evil spirits.

In this book I will tell you many things that may seem extreme at first, but let me assure you that every incident I relate is just as God showed it to me.

In these revelations I saw dirty, slimy spirits that continually tried to harm me, but they could not because I was in the presence of Jesus and covered by His blood.

I saw other forms of unclean spirits that appeared on the surface to be beautiful, but I could feel the evil, and I knew that they were servants of Satan.

But how did the evil underworld come into being? I wondered. *Where did Satan come from? How were these creatures created, and what is their ultimate purpose?*

Before we talk about this, I want to relate to you an incident that took place during one of my visits to hell.

A PICTURE OF THE LOST

I saw a woman in that place of the doomed. She was on her knees in a pit, as if looking for something. Her bones were showing through her dress, and her skeletal form was full of holes. Her dress was on fire. Her head was bald, and there were only holes where her eyes and nose were supposed to be.

A small fire burned around her feet where she was kneeling, and she clawed the sides of the brimstone pit. The fire clung to her hands, and dead flesh kept falling off as she dug.

Tremendous sobs shook her body. "O Lord, O Lord," she cried, "I want out."

As I watched, she finally got to the top of the pit with her feet. I thought she was going to get out when a large demon came rushing at her.

He had great wings that seemed to be broken at the top hanging down his sides. His color was brownish-black, and he had hair all over his large form. His eyes were set far back into his head, and he was about the size of a large grizzly bear.

The demon ran up to the woman. I saw him push her backward very hard into the pit and the fire. In horror I watched her falling.

I felt so sorry for her. I wanted to take her into my arms and hold her, to ask God to heal her and take her out of there.

Jesus knew my thoughts and said, "My judgment has been set. God has spoken. Even when she was a child, I called and called her to repent. I pleaded with her to serve Me. When she was sixteen years old, I called her to come follow Me, but she would not listen. She said, 'Someday I will serve You. I have no time for You now. Tomorrow, I will come.' Sadly, tomorrow never came for her; she waited too long."

The woman looked up at Jesus so longingly and said, "My sweet Lord, if only I had listened to You! Satan used my beauty and my money, and all my thoughts turned to how much power he would give me.

"Even then, God continued to draw me. But I thought, *I have tomorrow or the next day.* Then one day while I was riding in a car, the driver ran off the road, and I was killed almost instantly."

She begged, "Lord, please let me out."

As she spoke, her bony hands and arms reached out to Jesus while the flames continued to burn her. Jesus said, "The judgment is set."

VITAL LESSONS TO BE LEARNED

I was crying inside about the horrors of hell. I was seeing firsthand the agonies and torment of the lost souls there. "Dear Lord," I cried, "the torment is too real. When a soul comes here, there is no hope. There is no life. There is no love. Hell is too real."

Jesus impressed in my heart the importance of learning how evil spirits operate on earth if we are to escape that place where there is only pain and suffering and where there are no tomorrows.

That is what this book is about.

Chapter 2

The Origin of Evil

As I recall all the many revelations God has shown me, I am overwhelmed by the simple fact that Jesus is so good and His mercy is so great. He loves the world so much! God does not want a single person to be lost (2 Peter 3:9).

Surely, God is good. He is nothing but good. Everything He does is only good. Everything He makes is perfect in every way. Unlike what some people say, the cosmos did not appear suddenly from some vague, mystical "big bang."

I believe that the Word of God is true. I believe that in the beginning *"God created the heavens and the earth"* (Genesis 1:1 NKJV).

THE CREATION OF SPIRITS

At some undisclosed point in eternity, after the creation of the universe, God, in His infinite wisdom, created *all spirit beings.*

The apostle Paul said about Jesus,

> [16] By him were all things created, that are in heaven, and that are in earth, visible and invisible, whether they be thrones, or dominions, or principalities, or powers: all things were created by him, and for him.
>
> (Colossians 1:16)

Thus we see that God created all spirits, both the angels of light and those that rebelled against Him. The psalmist talked about the creation of angels:

> [2] Praise ye him, all his angels: praise ye him, all his hosts.
>
> [5] Let them praise the name of the LORD: for he commanded, and they were created. (Psalm 148:2, 5)

Certainly the Lord created angels, but did He really create demons? I often wondered. *Did He create the devil himself? And where did evil spirits come from?*

Unquestionably, spirit creatures are the highest order of created beings. The Bible says that humans are made *"a little lower than the angels"* (Hebrews 2:7). Yet, man is to have dominion over everything that God has created. (See Genesis 1:28.)

Spirit beings are not restricted and confined by flesh and blood as humans are.

I began to realize as I saw these revelations that spirits are intelligent beings who have understanding and emotions. In no way did angels or demons ever appear to me to be robots, unfeeling and blindly obeying some command.

All of the angels I saw willingly and immediately obeyed God always. They seemed to me to have the ability to choose between options.

Demons, on the other hand, originally opted to follow the instructions of the evil spirits immediately over them in the satanic hierarchy. It was apparent to me that they have no choice now but to obediently follow orders.

THE KINGDOM OF DARKNESS

This insight into the nature of spirit beings helped me to see more clearly the nature of evil and Satan.

That evil one, Satan, had a choice in the aeons past to continue in his allegiance to God or to rebel against Him. He chose to rebel and to lead other angels in doing so also. He began to deliberately oppose God.

God showed me that in their original created states, all spirit beings were holy angels or some form of angelic creatures.

All inhabitants of the evil underworld, those spirits of darkness, are aware of the fact that God is their Creator. But they hate God and His work.

When the Lord revealed these things to me, Jesus caught me up with Him, and I was transported to a place where I could see the kingdom of darkness and evil spirits.

BACK IN TIME

During one of these experiences, I was shown a beautiful being that looked like an archangel.

"His name is Lucifer," Jesus said. "He is called the son of the morning because of his beauty and his influence."

As I gazed at him, I saw a ghastly change come over his countenance and his entire being.

Suddenly and without warning, he was expelled from heaven and found himself wandering through space in confusion and disarray.

"What you are seeing happened many, many years ago," Jesus informed me. "Because he was so beautiful and well-loved, Lucifer allowed pride to germinate in his heart, and he rebelled against God. He thought he could overthrow the Mighty One."

> [12] How art thou fallen from heaven, O Lucifer, son of the morning! how art thou cut down to the ground, which didst weaken the nations!
>
> [13] For thou hast said in thine heart, I will ascend into heaven, I will exalt

my throne above the stars of God: I will sit also upon the mount of the congregation, in the sides of the north:

¹⁴ I will ascend above the heights of the clouds; I will be like the most High.

¹⁵ Yet thou shalt be brought down to hell, to the sides of the pit.

(Isaiah 14:12-15)

REBELLION IN HEAVEN

"No!" I protested, "No one—nothing—can be a rival to God!"

"So Lucifer found out," Jesus explained. "But before he did, he convinced other angels in heaven to join his rebellion. They renounced their allegiance to God.

"They cast away all goodness and began to take on all the characteristics that are opposite to the nature of God. They took on pride. They began to be arrogant. They took on haughtiness. They began to exalt themselves. They began to exalt and worship Satan instead of Me.

"Lucifer was cast out of heaven and became Satan, the accuser," Jesus said.

[9] And the great dragon was cast out, that old serpent, called the Devil, and Satan, which deceiveth the whole world: he was cast out into the earth, and his angels were cast out with him.

[10] And I heard a loud voice saying in heaven, Now is come salvation, and strength, and the kingdom of our God, and the power of his Christ: for the accuser of our brethren is cast down, which accused them before our God day and night.

(Revelation 12:9-10)

HOSTILITY AGAINST MAN

Since that time, Satan has been doing all he can to wreck Planet Earth where God created man in His own image.

Although Satan himself is foul and deeply depraved, he constantly brags and boasts about what he calls his own "perfections." Satan, as an archangel and one of the sons of the morning, no doubt possessed a breadth and depth of knowledge and understanding that is completely incomprehensible to us. His strength was equal to his knowledge. His deceit surpassed both his knowledge and his strength. Yet, he boasts because he is full of envy.

All unclean spirits are full of envy. They envy God, for Satan himself aspired after the throne of God. They envy the good spirits, the angels of God, who enjoy the heaven from which the evil spirits fell. And they envy born-again Christians who are called to inherit the kingdom of God.

Unclean spirits are filled with rage and cruelty against all the children of men. They long to motivate every person to commit the same wickedness that they themselves practice.

They want to involve all people everywhere in their own misery.

DEMONIC FORCES

With my own eyes I saw countless multitudes of evil spirits and demons of all descriptions. I was overwhelmed with their number, and asked the Lord, "How many evil spirits and demons exist?"

"More than you can count," He told me.

Nevertheless, I understood that the number of demons is not infinite. I don't know how many exist; God alone knows what the figure is. Without a doubt, the number is staggering.

"No wonder Your people on earth are being bombarded by hell!" I blurted before I realized what I was saying.

"Remember, My child," He rebuked me gently. *'Greater is he that is in you, than he that is in the world'"* (1 John 4:4). "Your help is My Spirit and My power and My angels. Righteous forces can never be defeated!"

WAR IN THE HEAVENS

We read this passage in Revelation:

> [4] And his tail drew the third part of the stars of heaven, and did cast them to the earth....
>
> [7] There was war in heaven: Michael and his angels fought against the dragon; and the dragon fought and his angels,
>
> [8] and prevailed not; neither was their place found any more in heaven.

> ⁹ And the great dragon was cast out, that old serpent, called the Devil, and Satan, which deceiveth the whole world: he was cast out into the earth, and his angels were cast out with him.
>
> (Revelation 12:4, 7–9)

Verse four says that a third of the angels joined the devil's rebellion. I will say more about this in another chapter, but I want you to understand that these fallen, evil angels or demons do not wander around without purpose.

They are united under a common leader. That leader is Satan.

- 📖 Jesus called Satan *"the prince of this world"* three times (John 12:31, 14:30, 16:11).
- 📖 Paul called Satan *"the god of this world"* (2 Corinthians 4:4).
- 📖 Satan is the great *"adversary"* (1 Peter 5:8) of both God and man.
- 📖 Jesus often called him *"the devil,"* a word that means "slanderer."
- 📖 Jesus called this slanderer *"a murderer"* and *"a liar, and the father of it"* (John 8:44).

📕 The Bible calls Satan *"the angel of the bottomless pit"* and *"Apollyon,"* or destroyer (Revelation 9:11).

📕 The Bible calls Satan a *"serpent"* (2 Corinthians 11:3) who, using trickery, seduced Eve in the Garden of Eden.

ORGANIZED CONSPIRACY

As I saw our arch-enemy organizing his evil forces, taking reports, giving orders, planning strategy, and motivating his workers to do more, I observed him trying to hinder every good word and trying to frustrate every good work of the kingdom of God. If he cannot convince a person to do evil, he will do everything possible to keep him or her from doing good.

What pains he takes to thwart and prevent the general work of God!

I saw his evil spirits work diligently to hinder the Word of God from being spread to the hearts of men. I was amazed at the many devices hell uses to stop the progress of redemption and maturity in the souls of God's people.

Constant attempts are made to hinder the continuing growth of believers in the knowledge of our Lord Jesus Christ!

TRAPPED BY THE SNARES OF THE ENEMY

A precious child of God who once fell victim to the devil's wicked schemes wrote to me, detailing the depths of her despair and her long journey to personal and divine freedom. She admitted that it was her pride, self-will, and disobedience that caused her to fall deeply into the snare of the devil. For a while it seemed to her that there was no way out. Alcohol, tobacco, drugs, and every form of sin and degradation became a constant part of her daily life.

As a result of her disobedience, her mind slipped. She was finally confined to a solitary cell in a hospital, and the memories of the past were blotted from her mind.

But, thank God, He heard her prayers and delivered her from every unclean spirit.

Here is the marvelous testimony she wrote:

A Testimony of Escape

Every night, devils came to me and tormented me. Satan himself stood before me and said, "God is not real! He is only a myth. Jesus is not real."

Satan stood there, and his eyes were like coals of fire. He seemed to look right through me and into my soul. Then he laughed and said in a voice like thunder, "I am the ruler of this world. Many are following me. I don't have to torment or possess them. They are already mine.

"But I desire to make people like you anxious to do my every bidding. Then I will be like God, having my throne and people to bow and worship me."

That fiend from hell pointed an ominous finger at me and said, "I want you and your precious treasure. I have stolen treasures from others for my glory.

"I need your treasure also to add to my glory. I want to be more glorious and more powerful than your miserable God.

"He is not beautiful. Why do you serve Him? I am just as powerful as He is. Come, while there is time. Do not hate me! Serve me."

"Me? Serve you?" I cried. "You who have destroyed my happiness? You who have made me a lonely creature and my soul as dry and desolate as the desert? You who have brought only sickness and woe to all who serve you? You who rule the darkness of this world and destroy all happiness and hope? You who have a lake of fire awaiting those who follow after you?

"No!" I screamed. "I will not serve you, most terrible evil one. Go away from me! Depart and never torment me anymore. The blood be upon you and your demons!"

The Venom of Satan's Rage

In a raging anger, Satan cried, "I will make you miserable, weakling. You can cry blood, but without power it is only a word. And you haven't the power now or ever. I am too big for you. Just a little longer, and I will have you completely.

"Not just my helpers, but I, Lucifer, the son of the morning, the most beautiful of all, will possess you. You are helpless against me.

"My wrath has been kindled against you. You will never be a good Christian, for I am stronger than the Most High.

"You will be so miserable when I get through with you that you will be glad to serve me, worship me, and adore me.

"I, Lucifer, son of the morning, most handsome of all the angels, have spoken."

Then he vanished just as the sun was dawning. All night, the devil had spoken to me. His words stayed with me, so that I am able to write the main thoughts to you, using his own words, just as he spoke them to me that night.

God must have a work for me to do that will hinder Satan's work greatly.

Deadly Beauty

Her testimony continued: Satan is not an ugly thing with horns, a pitchfork, and a long pointed tail. He was beautiful. He had on a lovely robe.

His countenance was beautiful, but his eyes were evil. They looked like the eyes of a snake. And they were fascinating like a snake's eyes.

What a smooth talker he was at first! When I talked back to him, it infuriated him.

His proud body was straight. His robe was crimson, and his hair was like gold. His hands were smooth like a woman's hands. Pretty sandals graced his feet. They were made of gold, and the belt around his waist was, too.

The devil was a beautiful creature. But there was a feeling of evilness about him. His motions were suggestive, not like those of an angel from God.

The instant I saw this big, beautiful angel, I knew it was Satan, even before he opened his mouth. He was the most beautiful creature I have ever seen.

The Bible says that he was once the most beautiful angel in heaven. And even though he is evil personified, he still is able to transform *"himself into an angel of light"* (2 Corinthians 11:14 NKJV).

He has a cunning, honey-coated tongue. He can charm with his speech. The idea of a devil with horns and the like is just man's conception of something "devilish."

A Vision of Freedom

But God delivered me from Satan! The Lord showed me in a vision how I was led out by tender hands from the ensnarement of the evil one.

In my vision, as I wandered through a dark and dangerous wasteland, gaping chasms opened on every side. Oppressive fog concealed unknown pitfalls. Again and again, my feet almost slipped.

Then an unseen hand seemed to clasp mine. It led me back safely and unerringly to solid ground.

Although the environment about me was desolate, I could see a land of green pastures and fruitful trees in the distance. The clouds and darkness were left behind.

By God's hand, I was completely and totally delivered! I had fought my way through many miles of desolate wilderness. Satan and his demons had bid for my life, but God's bid was higher.

God has paid a great price for my freedom. He paid the price not of silver and gold, but of the precious blood of the Son of God.

A PERSONAL PLEA

My dear friends, as I read this heart-breaking, yet victorious letter, the Lord showed me many people all over America and around the world who are in bondage to Satan.

Some are called insane. Many have never heard that they can be delivered. This is why God has called me to write these things about the kingdom of darkness. It is easier to overcome Satan if we understand the way he works and what it takes to receive divine deliverance.

If you are being tormented by Satan, you can be delivered through the power of Jesus Christ and through the power of the Holy Spirit. The first step is to receive Him in faith and call in earnest on the name of Jesus!

Chapter 3

Star Wars: The Fight in the Heavens

All angels were created holy, but about one-third of them rebelled against God and fell from their exalted position. The Bible tells the story:

> [9] And the great dragon was cast out, that old serpent, called the Devil, and Satan, which deceiveth the whole world: he was cast out into the earth, and his angels were cast out with him. (Revelation 12:9)

Satan is the leader of all the "bad" or "fallen" angels. And he is a still a liar, a murderer, and a thief. (See John 8:44 and 10:10.)

The only demons he does not control are those locked up in *"chains of darkness"* (2 Peter 2:4). In another chapter I will relate to you what God showed me about them.

In fact, there are four references in the Gospels where Satan is called *"the ruler of the demons"* (Matthew 9:34, 12:24; Mark 3:22; Luke 11:15 [all NKJV]).

Jesus showed me that Satan was one of the archangels before he fell. As the *"son of the morning"* (Isaiah 14:12) before he fell, Lucifer had a breadth and depth of understanding incomprehensible to mere mortals. His power and strength were equal to his knowledge. Even after he fell, although he lost so much, he still retained some of his abilities as *"the prince of this world"* (John 12:31).

"Why do Satan and the evil spirits sometimes appear to be smarter and more alert spiritually than the people of earth?" I asked at one point.

"Demons are spirit-beings by nature," Jesus said, "and this makes them supernaturally brilliant."

THE WISDOM OF GOD

Jesus went on to say, "But the child of God who has been born again and who depends on the Holy Spirit for spiritual knowledge is more than a match in intelligence for any evil spirit, because he or she is anointed and led by My wisdom!"

Then I remembered the apostle Paul writing that the world in its wisdom did not know God, yet even the foolish things of God put to shame the wise of this world:

> [21] For after that in the wisdom of God the world by wisdom knew not God, it pleased God by the foolishness of preaching to save them that believe.
>
> [25] Because the foolishness of God is wiser than men; and the weakness of God is stronger than men.
>
> [26] For ye see your calling, brethren, how that not many wise men after the flesh, not many mighty, not many noble, are called:
>
> [27] But God hath chosen the foolish things of the world to confound the wise; and God hath chosen the

weak things of the world to con-
found the things which are mighty;

[28] And base things of the world, and
things which are despised, hath
God chosen, yea, and things which
are not, to bring to nought things
that are:

[29] That no flesh should glory in his
presence.

[1 Corinthians 1:21, 25-29]

I rejoiced in my God because I knew
that the saints are safe in Christ as long
as they trust in Him. I knew that if I let
Jesus fight my battles for me, I would
come out victorious every time.

THE MASTER MASQUERADER

"One of the reasons Satan outsmarts
some people is that they don't recognize
his disguises," the Lord told me. "He is a
master deceiver, and he always camou-
flages himself and his purposes until he
wants to reveal himself."

I saw Satan disguised in many different ways and forms, but I always recognized him because all the other spirits of
evil respected him and slavishly obeyed

him. Sometimes he looked like a roaring lion, prowling the earth and seeking prey he could devour (1 Peter 5:8). At other times he was beautiful and suave, appearing before the world as an angel of light (2 Corinthians 11:14).

ATMOSPHERE OF EVIL

I came to understand that Satan is a cruel dictator. He hates God with a passion—and he hates God's people just as much.

Satan and his evil demons are behind the current unrest that our society is experiencing. One of their primary goals is to create so much turmoil through deceit that people will get their eyes off God or will actually turn away from Him.

The Holy Spirit is moving through powerful revival, but the spiritual underworld is working frantically to oppose it.

DISCERNING EVIL

Scripture tells us to try or test the spirits to see if they are from God:

> [1] Dear friends, do not believe every spirit, but test the spirits to see whether they are from God, because many false prophets have gone out into the world.   (1 John 4:1 NIV)

How can we do this? How can we distinguish the spirits of evil, with all of their disguises, from the good spirits?

I have found out that evil spirits are on the side against God and righteousness in every dispute. If a spirit attempts to hinder the work of God, it is always an evil spirit. If a spirit focuses on a personality instead of focusing on the Word of God and on Jesus Christ, that spirit is always from the devil and from hell.

In this kingdom of darkness that was revealed to me, I saw beings that were almost beyond the human imagination. Although usually invisible to the natural human eye, many of these creatures appeared to me to be hideous and grotesque when I saw them with my spiritual eyes.

They work constantly against everything that is good and right. They are cruel in their tactics and malicious in their motives.

Demons are responsible for the widespread sin and degradation we see in the world today. Plagues such as alcoholism and sexual perversion are the works of these evil demons and fallen angels.

SPIRITS AT WORK

The Lord allowed me to see evil spirits giving instructions to individuals in all kinds of movements and cults. I noticed that New Age cultists and Satanists were especially receptive to these messages.

I witnessed evil spirits communicate their evil wishes and desires to people through thoughts and impressions. All who were held in the bondage of Satan—young and old—heeded the evil one.

I saw Satan marshal his deceitful, unclean spirits and commission them to carry out his diabolical schemes. I saw some of them influencing unsuspecting souls to partake of drugs of all kinds.

I watched unclean spirits go into many homes that were not under the protection of the blood of the Lamb of God, Jesus Christ. At the very least, they caused division and strife between spouses. These demons influenced others to abuse their children and their mates.

I could see people practicing all kinds of immorality openly and without shame. They were constantly being encouraged and prompted by unclean spirits.

I saw many people turn to the occult as an alternative to belief in God. They were being motivated by the passionate fervor of demons. Starting with "harmless" superstition, Satan would convince them that there was nothing wrong with dabbling in the occult.

In my revelations I saw spiritualists performing ritualistic rites and doing evil things. They practiced contacting the dark world with rituals, chants, spells, and seances. I saw them attempting to communicate with the dead.

I saw voodoo priests, shamans, witches, and other mediums lead so many hungry, seeking souls astray that they organized into covens. In every major city in the United States, Satan himself is worshipped.

The Lord let me see satanic churches sprinkled all across the United States of America and the people who gather to worship the devil in those places.

I saw evil spirits hanging around musical groups. It is a well-known fact that some popular rock groups have adopted names for themselves and their groups from satanic ritual. The words of many of the contemporary popular songs they write reflect their satanic influence.

SATAN IS REAL

Why do people do these things, especially things they know are wrong? Because they dabbled with the forbidden until they got caught in the enemy's trap and couldn't stop. The spirit world is real, my friend, and believers cannot afford to play around with the devil's toys.

Satan is real. To deny his existence would be to deny the truth of the Bible.

When the Lord was tempted in the wilderness, He demonstrated how we should behave toward the devil. When Satan demanded that Jesus worship him, the Savior replied:

> [10] For it is written, Thou shalt wor-
> ship the Lord thy God, and him only
> shalt thou serve.   [Matthew 4:10]

THE WORSHIP OF SATAN FORBIDDEN

God Himself recognized the power of evil and satanism by banning witches and mediums in the Old Testament. His people were forbidden to seek after them. They were repeatedly told to leave witchcraft alone.

> [6] The soul that turneth after such
> as have familiar spirits, and after
> wizards, to go a whoring after
> them, I will even set my face
> against that soul, and will cut him
> off.   [Leviticus 20:6]

God told Isaiah what would happen to people who wanted him to seek advice from the dead, which is essentially seeking out and contacting evil spirits:

> [19] When men tell you to consult
> mediums and spiritists, who whis-
> per and mutter, should not a peo-
> ple inquire of their God? Why
> consult the dead on behalf of the
> living?

[20]...If they do not speak according to this word, they have no light of dawn.

[21]...When they are famished, they will become enraged and, looking upward, will curse their king and their God.

[22] Then they will look toward the earth and see only distress and darkness and fearful gloom, and they will be thrust into utter darkness. (Isaiah 8:19–22 NIV)

God showed me the demon forces that cause witchcraft. I saw that they are the source of witchcraft of every form.

He showed me that Satan and his organization are the motivating influence behind every palm reader, fortune-teller, witch, warlock, superstition, evil spirit, and magic art. Black magic, voodooism, and animism are expressions of evil religious rites put in different forms. They are spawned by the forces of hell.

ANGELS WHO FELL

The fallen angels who followed after Lucifer and were cast out of heaven with him are just as full of pride and ambition

as their master. They often attach themselves to a person here on earth in order
to sow their seeds of discontent, disobedience, and depravity here.

Some talk about the New Age movement. Others boast of the human poten-
tial movement. Some resort to what is
called channeling. But the leading advo-
cates of these so-called "new" religions
are merely the same old sorcerers oper-
ating under new names.

God showed me that even some of
His precious children are being duped by
evil spirits. These unwary souls allow
something to persuade them to purchase
pieces of supposedly magical crystal and
place them in their homes or offices.
Some even wear these charms around
their necks, hoping for power or healing.

Jesus said to me, "It makes me sad
when I see believers resort to doing some
of the very same things that the people
of the world do as a matter of course."

Now, let me give you the testimony of
a fellow believer who was attacked by
Satan in a terrible way. Jesus gave him
the victory, but the triumph was not
gained without a terrific fight. Here is

the story of an embattled pastor as he related it to me:

TORTURING THE SAINTS

I was worn and weary in body. I had been under a load mentally and was undergoing considerable and unbelievable nervous strain.

We were nearing the completion of an extended building program in the church, in addition to the constant daily demands of a busy pastor's life. The struggle had been a long and hard one.

When this thing attacked me, I was on the very verge of physical exhaustion. This was the reason leaders and many of the members of my church insisted that I needed a rest and a change of scenery.

I had retired for the night and was lying upon my bed, weary and tired, but I was restless and couldn't go to sleep.

Suddenly the thing seemed to attack me in the very pit of my stomach. From there it followed certain courses down to the very tips of my toes and fingers.

At first, it was just sort of an uneasy feeling. Gradually, its intensity increased until it became a tormenting sensation that I could not ignore.

As it went down into my fingers and toes, it felt as though some force was snapping my toes and my fingers off at the joints. I could find no position for my body that would ease the horrible strain and torment even for a moment.

Then, the thing began to retrace the same courses from my fingers and toes back through my body to the original starting point, the pit of my stomach.

As it progressed, it seemed that every part of my body was seized with horrible, agonizing pain. The tormenting pain became intense. I felt that if it became any worse my body would literally fly into a million pieces. I was in agony. I was being tormented.

A Struggle with Spirits

At the time I did not know what was tormenting me. My church friends told me I was suffering a nervous breakdown, and I believed them. Leaders in the church prayed for me, but their prayers seemed to help only for a few moments.

As soon as they were gone, the agony was as severe as ever. I felt sure that if it became any worse, I would not be able to restrain myself from tearing my hair out.

Many times I buried my face in my pillow to smother the screams I could not suppress. This condition lasted for two weeks, day and night, without relief, with long, agonizing, sleepless nights.

The days didn't seem quite so filled with anguish. Although I was so weak from pain that I could barely move, I repeatedly got up and paced the floor.

At the suggestion of close friends in the church, I was persuaded to get away and go for a much-needed vacation and rest. After I was several days and many miles away from the labors and activities of my pastorate, I still found no relief from this thing that constantly tormented my soul.

High in the mountains, I rented a beautiful little cabin. For a week I spent my days climbing mountains, trying to wear myself out so that when night came, I would go to sleep.

But I spent dark hours lying there in bed, suffering torment worse than death, wondering why I couldn't sleep. I knew that my condition was not improving, but rather growing worse.

A Demon of Fear

Fear began to take hold of me. I wondered if I was going insane. Was I losing my mind? Was I going to "crack up"? Would I snap under the strain, as other people I knew had done?

Surely, a man couldn't stand much more of what I was going through! I felt certain that at any moment my mind would snap under the terrible strain and torment.

A thousand times a day I wondered what would happen to me if I experienced a complete nervous collapse. Would I die? Would I go insane? Would I be committed to a psychiatric ward? Surely, no human being could continue like this much longer without literally going to pieces.

After a week way up in the mountains, I finally made up my mind that if I was going to be sick, I would be sick where I had friends and family, not alone in some mountain cabin. So I decided to go back home.

I thought that driving would surely bring on drowsiness. If I drove all day, I reasoned, I should be so completely exhausted that when I stopped for the night, I would fall asleep almost immediately.

But I found that when a person is being tormented, he is not capable of exhausting himself to the point of bringing about natural, restful sleep.

After driving all day long, I stopped for the night, only to spend it rolling and tossing restlessly on a bed, wondering if the next minute would be my last. I knew the time had come when my nerves could no longer endure the strain.

In the afternoon of the third day, I was driving through a large city in the Midwest. As I drove away from it, God began to reveal to me exactly what was tormenting me.

The Lord let me know that although my condition had something to do with my nerves, and my nerves had something to do with my condition, there was something more involved.

A Demon of Torment

I was being viciously tormented by a demon that was assailing me through my nerves, just as an infirm spirit attacks a person's eyes and causes blindness, or his ears and causes deafness, or his joints and causes him to be crippled.

The truth suddenly dawned on me as though Christ Himself had preached an enlightening sermon for me alone. No wonder I couldn't sleep at night! No wonder I was unable to wear myself out sufficiently to bring about sleep. It was not with myself that I was at war.

My problem was not my nerves. I was at war with an unseen force, the very force of the devil himself. When I finally realized the truth of these facts, I knew what I had to do to win the victory.

And I did it! I sought the help of a Christian friend. Explaining to him what God had revealed to me, I asked for his prayers.

As we began to pray and rebuke that foul, tormenting devil, commanding him to go, I could feel something in the pit of my stomach begin to flutter. It seemed like a bird in a cage, fluttering wildly, trying to find a way out. But it seemed that the cage was closed, and the bird couldn't get out.

Then we commanded, "In Jesus' name, you GO!" Suddenly, the door to the cage was opened. In a split second the thing that tormented me was gone! It was gone forever! It had been cast out!

My thoughts turned to the thousands of other people who, in like circumstances, resorted to treatments, cures, and specialists—all to no avail! How happy I was that God had let me know my true condition. How happy I was that I could face facts and win the victory. I began to rejoice.

You, Too, Can Be Free

What an outstanding testimony from a blessed servant of God this is! The man who gave me this testimony wants us to know that only through Jesus Christ is there victory over the devil and all the forces of hell.

Perhaps you, too, are being tormented by a similar spirit. Maybe you are tired all the time, and Satan is telling you that it will never be any better for you. You may be nervous, or near the breaking point. The cares of life may be too heavy for you.

But the good news is that you can be free! You can win the victory over all of the forces of hell!

The horrible fear that grips you night and day, the overwhelming compulsion that controls you, the voices that you hear, the forms that you see—these are all real. But they are the realities of hell!

Jesus is more powerful than all evil forces combined. To be delivered, you must first face the fact that these things are satanically inspired and are evil spirits.

You must understand that your condition is a part of the spiritual warfare that is going on between the forces of God and the forces of Satan.

Then you must come to Christ in faith. Name your compulsion what it is. Call your addiction by its right name. Confess whatever your stumbling block is to God, and admit that you need help.

You will find Him there for you!

Chapter 4

Lucifer, the Liar

In the glorious revelations from God, He showed me that there are people today who are actually possessed by demons. Many more are dominated, influenced, controlled, and directed by demons without actually being possessed by them.

God also disclosed to me people who are so *oppressed* and vexed by the spirits of evil that they do not seem to be very different from those who are *possessed* by them.

The Lord taught me that because Lucifer lusted after the glory and adoration God receives from the angels, he conceived, planned, and executed a cosmic rebellion. Satan fully intended to replace God's rulership of the universe with his own.

Like many people today, Lucifer did not believe that God would or could react effectively to what he thought was a perfectly planned rebellion. His attitude was expressed in the words of Eliphaz the Temanite:

> 13 What does God know? Does he judge through such darkness?
>
> 14 Thick clouds veil him, so he does not see us as he goes about in the vaulted heavens.
>
> (Job 22:13-14 NIV)

Despite Satan's cleverness, however, he was wrong about God. Our loving Father responded in a way that would fulfill His perfect standard of righteousness without compromising His holy character. His eternal purpose was, and still is, to restore perfection and completeness to His universe.

God revealed to me the fallen angels who had become lost spirits, roaming the cosmos and obeying Satan's orders. I saw them working constantly against the plan and will of God.

How Satan Uses People

X   I saw Satan passionately instruct those angels who fell with him. He urged the ranks of wicked spirits to awaken every evil passion, every evil thought, and every evil temper in every heart that they could.

I saw these demons as they longed to inhabit physical bodies. God showed me that the urge to satisfy our natural physical desires is a part of the human condition that Satan exploits. He distorts and twists our desires into sin in order to thwart the work of the Lord in individuals and even in nations.

The psalmist perfectly described the ploy of the kingdom of darkness when he wrote this:

> 5 They encourage each other in evil plans, they talk about hiding their snares; they say, "Who will see them?"
>
> 6 They plot injustice and say, "We have devised a perfect plan!" Surely the heart and mind of man are

cunning.

7 But God will shoot them with arrows; suddenly they will be struck down.   (Psalm 64:5 – 7 NIV)

The New Testament teaches that a person can be demon possessed. When a person is dominated by the spirit of a demon and tormented by it, it may affect the person spiritually, physically, psychologically, or intellectually. The Lord revealed to me that some people are affected in all four ways.

The biblical accounts of Jesus' ministry to many afflicted people are clear illustrations that demon possession causes various kinds of sickness, insanity, leprosy, blindness, lameness, deafness, and other defects and diseases.

The Lord said that Satan's purpose is to fight against God and His work and that Satan is a liar. If Satan is a liar, so are his servants (John 8:44). If Satan is a deceiver (Revelation 12:9), so are they. If Satan comes to steal, kill, and destroy (John 10:10), so do they. Their purpose, always, is to thwart the work of God. (See Matthew 24:24, for example.)

Evil Spirits Are Destructive

Demons will torment and bind an individual until the person feels that he no longer has control and is not really his own.

In my visions I heard demons talk among themselves. I listened as they talked through the people they possessed. I heard them cry with loud voices as they used the lips and tongues of the people they were tormenting.

I could see demons standing, walking, and wandering about, seeking a place to rest. I saw them enter into the bodies of many people and into animals.

Then I remembered reading in the Bible about a person who had an entire legion of demons inside his body:

> [27] And when He stepped out on the land, there met Him a certain man from the city who had demons for a long time. And he wore no clothes, nor did he live in a house but in the tombs.
>
> [28] When he saw Jesus, he cried out, fell down before Him, and with a loud voice said, "What have I to

do with You, Jesus, Son of the Most High God? I beg You, do not torment me!"

29 For He had commanded the unclean spirit to come out of the man. For it had often seized him, and he was kept under guard, bound with chains and shackles; and he broke the bonds and was driven by the demon into the wilderness.

30 Jesus asked him, saying, "What is your name?" And he said, "Legion," because many demons had entered him.

31 And they begged Him that He would not command them to go out into the abyss.

32 Now a herd of many swine was feeding there on the mountain. So they begged Him that He would permit them to enter them. And He permitted them.

33 Then the demons went out of the man and entered the swine, and the herd ran violently down the steep place into the lake and drowned.

34 When those who fed them saw what had happened, they fled and told it in the city and in the country.

35 Then they went out to see what had happened, and came to Jesus,

and found the man from whom the demons had departed, sitting at the feet of Jesus, clothed and in his right mind. And they were afraid.

[36] They also who had seen it told them by what means he who had been demon-possessed was healed.

(Luke 8:27–36 NKJV)

This man had been truly possessed. In Mark 5:13, we read that the unclean spirits that were cast out of him went into a herd of swine and about two thousand pigs drowned in the sea.

I heard demons quoting Scripture and remembered that Satan quoted Psalm 91:11–12 to Jesus. (See Matthew 4:5–7.)

These spirits would tell lies in very cunning ways and convince their victims that the lies were true. Then the lying spirits would persuade them to repeat the lies to others.

HOW DEMONS AFFECT THEIR VICTIMS

In the biblical accounts of Jesus' ministry on earth, the gospel writers relate many incidents of demons occupying people's bodies. One story is about a young teenage boy who had been afflicted and tormented since he was a child:

> [17] Then one of the crowd answered and said, "Teacher, I brought You my son, who has a mute spirit.
>
> [18] "And wherever it seizes him, it throws him down; he foams at the mouth, gnashes his teeth, and becomes rigid. So I spoke to Your disciples, that they should cast it out, but they could not."
>
> [19] He answered him and said, "O faithless generation, how long shall I be with you? How long shall I bear with you? Bring him to Me."
>
> [20] Then they brought him to Him. And when he saw Him, immediately the spirit convulsed him, and he fell on the ground and wallowed, foaming at the mouth.
>
> [21] So He asked his father, "How long has this been happening to him?" And he said, "From childhood.
>
> [22] "And often he has thrown him both into the fire and into the water to destroy him. But if You can do anything, have compassion on us and help us."
>
> [23] Jesus said to him, "If you can believe, all things are possible to him

who believes."

[24] Immediately the father of the child cried out and said with tears, "Lord, I believe; help my unbelief!"

[25] When Jesus saw that the people came running together, He rebuked the unclean spirit, saying to it, "Deaf and dumb spirit, I command you, come out of him and enter him no more!"

[26] Then the spirit cried out, convulsed him greatly, and came out of him. And he became as one dead, so that many said, "He is dead."

[27] But Jesus took him by the hand and lifted him up, and he arose.

(Mark 9:17-27 NKJV)

I saw people who were demon possessed, just as this boy had been, actually fall to the ground, wallow around like animals, and foam at the mouth.

Once I saw a man making his halting way down a street, and several demons hovered around him. I understood that the spirits of blindness had caused the man to lose his sight.

On another occasion I saw what looked like a whole host of demons swarming around some people. As they became focused on an individual, I grew to understand that these were demons of deafness and that they were robbing the person of his hearing.

I saw mute spirits make people speechless, unable to speak.

I saw the spirits of lameness cripple and twist the limbs of their victims. As they bound these people physically, I could see that their terrible deeds caused the bodies of many to be horribly misshapen and disfigured.

Sometimes, I noticed that demons would motivate the people they possessed by shoving and poking, driving them toward destruction. At other times I would see the spirits leading an individual, often gently, the way they wanted him or her to go. At all times demons and evil spirits are cunning and deceitful.

Some evil spirits that I saw caused their victims to go naked. Under the influence of vile spirits, some people dressed suggestively, and others wore outlandish, attention-getting garments. These people did whatever it took to get other people to notice them.

In everything that demonic spirits do, their purpose is always to divert the focus from whatever is right. I often observed them carry on running conversations with the thoughts of the people they tormented.

More than once I watched in horror as I saw women as well as men take a gun, put it to their own bodies, and commit suicide. The Lord let me see that the act of suicide is prompted by demons and evil spirits, as hopeless souls follow the voices of hell that delude them. Those voices made them think that they were doing what was right.

Listen, friend, if a voice ever tells you to end it all, know that the voice is not from God. It is from Satan or from one of his demons. It is a complete lie of the enemy who is out to kill you. Jesus came so you *might have life* (John 10:10).

Spirits of jealousy can make a person obsessively jealous, miserable, and unable to find any personal peace. I saw a woman haranguing and ranting and nagging her husband because of an unreal jealousy. Jesus revealed to me that those demons of jealousy would destroy her home and her marriage unless she allowed Him to deliver her.

I saw demons causing people to do things they never intended to do. I saw intelligent, knowledgeable people in prison and confined to mental institutions. Jesus told me they were there because they yielded to the voice of Satan and demon forces overpowered them.

FIERCE FIGHTERS AGAINST THE GOOD

One thing became obvious to me as God showed me the big picture. As the demons inhabited human beings, I noticed a single truth: Once within a person, an evil spirit never willingly leaves.

When a servant of God casts a demon out of a person, the evil spirit always seeks to re-enter the same person or another being, preferably someone nearby. If spirits go back to the delivered person, they always take other demons with them. Jesus explained it like this:

> [21] When a strong man, fully armed, guards his own house, his possessions are safe.

²² But when someone stronger attacks and overpowers him, he takes away the armor in which the man trusted and divides up the spoils.

²⁴ When an evil spirit comes out of a man, it goes through arid places seeking rest and does not find it. Then it says, "I will return to the house I left."

²⁵ When it arrives, it finds the house swept clean and put in order.

²⁶ Then it goes and takes seven other spirits more wicked than itself, and they go in and live there. And the final condition of that man is worse than the first.

(Luke 11:21-22, 24-26 NIV)

An evangelist told about a young man who was possessed and tormented by a demon. The young man suddenly began causing a disturbance in church. Here is the evangelist's testimony:

DISTURBING THE PEACE

An usher came to me during the worship service and reported that a man in the back of the auditorium was "having a spell."

Only a few moments before, the young man had been sitting there with a songbook in his hand, enjoying the service, when suddenly he began to stiffen and lose control of himself. A spirit more powerful than his own took over his body, and it was not the Spirit of God.

I went immediately to find out what was causing the disturbance. But, before I could get back to the person, excitement had begun to mount. A rather large group had already gathered around him. Some saints were praying, while others plainly did not know what to do.

The young man's body was tensed and stretched out on a chair, and it took several strong men to hold him down. What a pitiful sight that was! Blood ran down from the man's mouth as he chewed his tongue. He was completely stretched out, writhing on the chair. Uncanny, animal-like sounds came from his mouth.

The scene had such an unreal, unearthly aura about it all.

The demon that had control of him was as real as the blood, the foaming lips, the chewed tongue, the writhing body, and the uncanny sounds I saw and heard.

But, thank God, the Spirit of the Lord, a stronger spirit, came down. As we ministered to him and rebuked the demons in the name of Jesus, the young man was completely delivered that night by the mighty power of God!

THE DECEIT OF THE EVIL ONE

Friends, God revealed to me that the devil will torment those he cannot destroy. If he cannot entice a person to sin, he will, so far as he is permitted, cause the person as much pain as he can.

While I beheld the workings of Satan and what he and his imps were doing to people, the Lord spoke a special message to my heart.

He told me that many of the pains of humanity that we often pass off lightly as nervousness are, in reality, the work of the diabolical forces of evil. Many of the accidents we dismiss as coincidental or inevitable are, in fact, the work of demons. What we sometimes call acts of nature or acts of God may, in truth, be the fiendish work of unclean spirits. This includes instances of storms, wind, blizzards, hail, lightning, and earthquakes.

My friend, if only you could realize the vast range of all the work of Satan and his demons! He makes himself known in every area of life. If only you could see the extent of his influence! The evil spirits of the spiritual underworld are the agents for more mischief and heartbreak that we could ever imagine.

But what appears on the surface often does not reveal the total picture. Satan is often responsible for marriages breaking up. He is frequently the reason for the recurring trouble from which you seemingly cannot escape.

THE WAY TO VICTORY

You cannot have peace as long as demons control your life. They will always lead you astray. They will direct your path away from God. When you are cleansed, you need the Holy Spirit to fill every corner of your life so that evil spirits have no place to dwell.

But God showed me that we can have the victory over every force of hell. Praise God, there is One who is stronger than Satan is.

My friend, when you are armed in your own strength, you are no match for the spirits of darkness. But when you are armed with the Holy Spirit and with spiritual armor, nothing can harm you in Christ.

Jesus Christ is my King! He is my Savior! His power is greater than all the powers of the evil underworld.

He is King of Kings and Lord of Lords. He has the keys to death, hell, and the grave (Revelation 1:18). He is my ever-present Champion!

If you have not committed your life to Him, now is the time to do it.

Chapter 5

Seven Realms of Spiritual Warfare

In the revelations God gave me of the vast spiritual arena, I saw the whole world and its atmosphere filled with devils and demons. They not only tried to control those people who were engaged in open idolatry, but also to influence every phase and form of life on earth.

I saw them controlling thrones and rulers and holding sway over government leaders. I observed them hovering around the cradles of infants and imposing their presence in homes for the elderly. I saw them slouching around the sin-darkened dens of iniquity and dancing at glitzy showplaces that served as a camouflage for satanic activity. I even saw some of the evil spirits going to church services.

The air was polluted by their filth, and the earth was rapidly decaying because of their evil works. Although I knew that the earth was, and is, the creation of God, it seemed to literally become a hell. With great alarm I cried out, "Jesus, how can we overcome these evil forces?"

"Do not be afraid, My child," He told me. His voice was the loveliest voice I have ever heard. "Don't you remember that the purpose for My coming to the earth was to destroy the works of the devil?" (See 1 John 3:8.)

"While demons help Satan tempt people to sin and have great destructive powers, they lose their power when they are confronted by My power. Just as demons have no choice but to obey Me, so also are they subject to those who continue My work in My name on earth."

A peace and a calm settled over me as He continued to talk to me and show me the seven realms of spiritual warfare in which we are engaged today.

Four of those realms are described in Ephesians:

> ¹² For our struggle is not against flesh and blood, but against the rulers [*principalities*, KJV], against the authorities [*powers*, KJV], against the powers [*the rulers*, KJV] of this dark world and against the spiritual forces of evil [*spiritual wickedness*, KJV] in the heavenly realms [*high places*, KJV].
>
> (Ephesians 6:12 NIV)

This verse describes the governmental structure of the satanic kingdom. The Lord showed me that the *"heavenly realms"* are listed in descending order of authority, starting with the most powerful, and are occupied by a vast multitude of evil spirit beings.

Satan himself is the chief ruler of all evil, and he has a hierarchy of spirits under him. All of the angels who joined Satan in his rebellion against God fell with him and are now completely demonic. They obey Satan and carry out his wishes. Satan is the ultimate authority and the supreme commander of evil.

THE REALM OF PRINCIPALITIES

The first region is the *realm of principalities*. This is the command post from which Satan rules.

God showed me spirit beings that were reporting to the throne of Satan on a regular basis. I watched as these evil agents cunningly helped design, plan, and carry out the wishes of Satan himself. I realized these were the chief spirits that control the realm of principalities.

Paul said we are first waging spiritual warfare against principalities or rulers. According to *Strong's Concordance*, the original Greek word that Paul wrote in Ephesians 6:12 means "first, primary, highest ranking, or chief," combined with "power, principality, magistrate, principle, or ruler." Thus, the realm of principalities is the highest level of Satan's government and has the greatest concentration of power, and Satan is the chief magistrate.

My friend, these things are not fantasies. They are very real. Satan has control over a powerful army that has as its primary goal the defeat of the church.

This army is made up of powerful fallen angels who have united under Satan and are vicious fighters. This is the leadership of the enemies we face. These principal rulers are the top generals in the fight, and they are shrewd and diligent.

THE REALM OF POWERS AND AUTHORITIES

The second-ranking realm in the demonic hierarchy is that of *powers and authorities.*

This realm as cited in Ephesians does not refer to human leadership of the world's governments. Instead, this region is occupied by evil spirits that have great power and authority, plus great destructive powers and abilities. They are the wrecking crew of the universe.

I saw Satan as he blessed these special evil spirits. I watched as he laid hands on the foul ones and sent them forth into the world to follow his instructions and to do their destructive work. I saw these special forces actually being energized and authorized by Satan as they returned to him periodically and reported the work they had done.

I gazed in fascination at the scenes being played out before me, and I listened intently to Jesus as He provided a running commentary on what was really happening. To hear Jesus' constant reassurance of victory for His own filled my heart with great zeal. I wanted to go immediately and tell the whole world what the Lord was showing to me.

Instead, He told me that I was to write these things in a book, just as I did in *A Divine Revelation of Hell* and *A Divine Revelation of Heaven*. These books have been read by millions of people, which says to me that, in these last days, people are very interested in spiritual matters and especially what lies ahead.

THE REALM OF THE RULERS OF DARKNESS

The third realm of spiritual enemies the Lord showed me is described in the Bible as *the realm of the rulers of this dark world.*

I saw the evil spirits in this realm constantly struggling and competing for spiritual territory. I understood that the unbelievable tension caused by these colossal struggles impacts humanity in a significant way.

Jesus told me that the spirit-prince of the kingdom of Persia that the archangel Michael talked about in Daniel was one of these rulers.

> [13] But the prince of the kingdom of Persia withstood me twenty-one days; and behold, Michael, one of the chief princes, came to help me, for I had been left alone there with the kings of Persia.
>
> [20] Then he said, "Do you know why I have come to you? And now I must return to fight with the prince of Persia; and when I have gone forth, indeed the prince of Greece will come." (Daniel 10:13, 20 NKJV)

This passage in Daniel suggests specific geographical boundaries where these particular spirit beings abide and work. Remember how the evil spirits ruled by the spirit called Legion in the demon-possessed man begged Jesus not to send them out of the region of Gadara. This is a confirmation by Jesus that certain demons are territorial in nature: *"Also* [Legion] *begged* [Jesus] *earnestly that He would not send them out of the country"* (Mark 5:10 NKJV).

The provinces of the world are committed to some of these rulers of darkness. While they seem to remain chiefly in the citadel of their kingdoms, however, other evil spirits roam about in the earth.

Some of the rulers of spiritual darkness are cultic demons. Others are rulers of this age, or culture demons. They specialize in influencing trends and the general atmosphere in society.

God showed me people who actually sacrifice to these devils and not to God. I saw men and women at a party, drinking and taking drugs. They were so stoned that they gladly welcomed the fellowship of the devil.

I saw it, friends—people who had pained looks on their faces, but they laughed and cursed, as filthy language came from their lips. They were all drinking from a large cup.

"Look, my child," Jesus said to me. "They are drinking from the cup of the devil. They are sitting at the devil's table." (See 1 Corinthians 10:20–21.)

THE REALM OF SPIRITUAL WICKEDNESS

Jesus told me that the phrase Paul used in Ephesians 6:12, *"spiritual wickedness in high places,"* does not refer to political escapades in some world capital. It does not describe some aura or atmosphere. Instead, it refers to the *realm of the spiritual forces of evil* of Satan's kingdom that operate in the heavenlies.

Jesus showed me that these diabolical spirits are the myriad of imps and demons that work day and night to carry out Satan's plans to destroy mankind and especially the church.

"Evil has even infiltrated the sacred ranks of My people," Jesus said, with sadness in His voice. "Some ministers offer no hope for those who seek grace and forgiveness. Choirs are crippled by discord. Lazy and lethargic laypeople fill too many pews. Too many drowsy deacons serve Me carelessly."

I saw that the wicked spirits who zealously follow the commands and instructions of Satan cause these things to happen.

The Lord Jesus revealed to me that not all demons roam about in the atmosphere above the earth. The largest group I saw, by far, were the evil spirits of Satan. They torment and tantalize people. They tempt and taunt God's chosen ones. They are your enemies and my enemies. We must always exercise the authority of Christ over them.

THE REALM OF THE HEART

The fifth arena for fighting the battle with evil spirits is the *realm of the heart*. "I will show you how Satan battles for the hearts of people," Jesus told me. "Battles with Satan must first be won in the heart."

Suddenly, I was transported back to earth and began to observe people. As they acted out their evil thoughts and desires, the Lord let me see that those things came from an inner conflict of their spirits with the unseen and unclean spirits of Satan.

The more people would give into the evil spirits who hounded them, the more they would ignore and disregard the voice of God. They failed to listen to the inner spiritual urges within them.

Temptation

One of the first tactics employed by these satanic messengers is *temptation*.

I saw many different forms of Satan's temptation. These allurements always appeared to be good or desirable, something pleasant that one would want to do.

Evil spirits are masters at enticing believers to do things that they know in their hearts are wrong. I saw them cause some of God's choice servants to wind up shipwrecked in their service for God.

Oppression

I heard these demonic spirits discussing their tactics. "If you cannot get someone to forget about God by temptation," one told his cohort, "use the wonderful weapon of *oppression*."

Many times I saw people carrying all kinds of difficulties and burdensome loads with great heaviness of spirit because they were oppressed by demon spirits. I began to understand that satanic oppression is one of the favorite tactics of our enemy. If he can, he will oppress you in spirit and take away all of your zest for daily living.

Obsession

I noticed that if temptation and oppression didn't work, these soldiers from hell would try *obsession*. They would try to get the person so obsessed with the occult and with demonology that these things were on his mind at all times. An obsessed person cannot focus on worshipping and serving God while thinking about devils and demons all the time.

Possession

The Lord stated emphatically that the worst stage of demonic activity is *demon possession.*

As demons and wicked spirits scurried about here and there, I noticed that they themselves were obsessed with possession. They wanted desperately to occupy human bodies.

In the Bible, several memorable examples are given of people being possessed by demons, as well as numerous other passages that mention evil spirits and their activities. In the New Testament we find the following:

- 📖 56 references to demons or devils
- 📖 6 references to evil spirits
- 📖 23 references to unclean spirits
- 📖 14 references to demon possession

"The forces of Satan always oppose God and His work," Jesus told me. "They do it every way they can by afflicting, opposing, hindering, and harassing Christians who are doing My work."

The activities of these deceitful and deceiving beings have probably increased, considering the fact that they know their time is short.

THE REALM OF THE MIND

Jesus told me that the sixth arena where spiritual warfare is waged is in the *realm of the mind.* He said that if the devil can interfere with a person's thought patterns, he has won a most important battle.

I remembered what the Word of God said: *"For as he thinks in his heart, so is he"* (Proverbs 23:7 NKJV).

The Lord said to me, "Just as My thoughts toward you are good, so Satan's thoughts are against you for evil. He will twist the words you say and try to confuse your thoughts. But with My Word in your heart, and with your mind constantly focused on Me, you can resist the devil."

The Lord brought to my mind some Scripture verses from the Word of God:

> [5] The thoughts of the righteous are right, but the counsels of the wicked are deceitful.
>
> (Proverbs 12:5 NKJV)

> [26] The thoughts of the wicked are an abomination to the LORD, but the words of the pure are pleasant.
>
> (Proverbs 15:26 NKJV)

> [3] Commit your works to the LORD, and your thoughts will be established. (Proverbs 16:3 NKJV)

THE REALM OF THE FLESH

God showed me that demons understand the flesh and its desires. This is why it is so important for believers to put on the whole armor of God and die to the flesh.

The Bible says, *"Put on the whole armor of God, that you may be able to stand against the wiles of the devil"* (Ephesians 6:11 NKJV).

Jesus showed me the many varied schemes and deceits of Satan. I am convinced that only by the power of the blood of Jesus and the Holy Spirit of God can a person be free and able to do God's work on earth as He wants us to.

Thank God, He frees us from the clutches of Satan and evil spirits. I heard my pastor, the Reverend Dr. T. L. Lowery, give this testimony about this very thing:

DELIVERED FROM DEMONS

In the early summer of 1981, I had just come off a forty-day fast during which I was seeking God's direction for the church. I was weak and frail in body, but felt good in my soul.

Almost immediately afterward, I received a telephone call inviting me to come and preach at the Alabama Camp Meeting in Birmingham. That night, as thousands of people filled the tabernacle, it seemed that there were just as many people standing and sitting around outside the building as there were inside.

When I stepped to the podium, I had to hold on to the pulpit in order to stand up. As I began to preach, I felt something come over me. People said that I looked as if I had seen a ghost. The congregation said that my countenance literally changed. I first thought this was because I was still experiencing the physical effects of the fast, but in reality it was the spiritual results of my fast.

The anointing of the Holy Spirit not only fell on me, but seemingly on everybody in the congregation. By the close of the message, it seemed that every able-bodied person in the tabernacle was standing. Hundreds came forward for salvation and to receive the baptism in the Holy Spirit.

In the prayer line for healing and deliverance, I saw a woman approach me and felt the Spirit check my spirit. When she reached where I was standing, I said to her, under the anointing of the Holy Spirit, "My dear lady, you are demon-possessed." Immediately, the look on her face changed, and her countenance became distorted in a horrible, grotesque manner.

I could hear the voice of the demon itself as the woman began to talk back to me. I put the microphone to her lips so that everyone at the camp meeting could hear what the demon was saying. The voice within her raged: "We've been here a long time, and we will not come out. You are powerless to force us to come out."

My spirit rose within me when she challenged the authority I have in Christ. The Spirit of God came on me stronger. The entire congregation heard me shout: "You foul demon of hell, you know who I am. I am T. L. Lowery, a servant of the living God; and I charge you in the name of Jesus Christ of Nazareth to come out! In Jesus' name, come out now!"

Suddenly, we heard an explosion that some said sounded like a cannon went off. The demon came out of the woman in a literal, physical manifestation. The people described it as a black, furry mass with a long tail. I saw it come out of the woman's mouth and shoot out over the heads of the people. Then it went out through the side of the tabernacle with a noise that sounded like a freight train.

Dramatically, before thousands of witnesses, the woman was wonderfully and gloriously delivered!

LIFE-CHANGING NEWS

The life-changing news today is that Jesus lives to gives us the victory over Satan and over all of his forces.

Satan is wise, but he is not all-wise. He has great power, but God's power is greater.

Many times I saw God thwart the plans of Satan and turn back his purposes as the people of God served faithfully and persevered in the midst of great difficulty.

Child of God, you can be assured that as long as you are covered by the blood of Jesus, demons and devils cannot touch you. You don't have to live in fear and defeat.

God has said that believers have the power to bind every form of evil they encounter. There is nothing that needs to have control over you. *"Sin shall not have dominion over you,"* Paul said, *"for you are not under law but under grace"* (Romans 6:14 NKJV). God's grace gives us the power to bind every evil force and every contrary authority that may come against us or attack us.

> [10] There shall no evil befall thee, neither shall any plague come nigh thy dwelling.
> [11] For he shall give his angels charge over thee, to keep thee in all thy ways.   (Psalm 91:10–11)

> [29] How can one enter a strong man's house and plunder his goods, unless he first binds the strong man? And then he will plunder his house.   (Matthew 12:29 NKJV)

> [19] And I will give you the keys of the kingdom of heaven, and whatever

> you bind on earth will be bound in
> heaven, and whatever you loose on
> earth will be loosed in heaven.
>
> (Matthew 16:19 NKJV)

God does not want you to be obsessed with demons or evil spirits. It is not His will for you. Be assured that Jesus has already defeated the enemy, and we are safe in Christ. We can be victorious over any demonic attacks.

Remember, God battles evil for us in all seven realms of spiritual warfare as we remain in Him.

Chapter 6

Evil Spirits and God's Power over Them

While Jesus was revealing to me how Satan and his forces operate, I noticed that the evil empire opposes the good on every occasion possible. In private homes and in public forums, they are arrayed against everything that is pure and righteous.

I witnessed demons defend everything filthy and nasty, especially those things condemned in the Word of God. They always opposed God and His ways. Their hideous figures and misshapen images, as they appeared to me, were matched only by their own filthy, evil, vile ways.

The Lord Jesus spoke to me and said, "If My people who trust in Me are armed with the knowledge of how the devil operates and what his strategies and tactics are, they can have power against the evil of this world."

The main motivation for me to write this book is to share the knowledge the Lord revealed to me about how to use all of the weapons God has given us as His children to defeat the enemy.

Jesus showed me that demons have only one interest in humans—to break down their minds, mentally; their souls, emotionally and psychologically; their bodies, physically; and their spirits, vitally. The sole objective for demonic spirits is to lead souls to hell or to cause people to do the very things that send them there.

I saw in my visions that demon possession is the outright control of a human personality by the power of a wicked spirit.

I saw demon powers working through soothsaying, fortune-telling, the occult, spiritism, spiritualism, and related black magic arts, such as astrology, tarot cards, voodooism, and New Age channeling.

As the world grows more and more godless and more and more secularized, demonic manifestations are increasing like a rising tide that is flooding our culture.

CHARACTERISTICS OF THE DEMON POSSESSED

As I saw the many people being tormented and possessed by devils, I began to notice certain characteristics about the people who yielded to the evil spirits or demons.

Dramatic Personality Differences

For one thing, demon-possessed people almost always undergo a *severe personality change*. Seeing this happen reminded me of the drastic behavior and personality changes that occur in a person who becomes totally under the influence of alcohol, only the changes with demon possession are much more pronounced and extreme. The power of the internal demons engulfs the possessed person's own identity and individuality. The person can no longer control himself and really does not care.

The passage in Mark 5:1–16 illustrates this point very clearly. The "before" and "after" descriptions of the demon-possessed man show that he was a completely different person when he was freed from demonic influence.

When Jesus asked the man for his name, the answer that came out of his mouth was *"My name is Legion, for we are many"* (v. 9), which demonstrated the personality of the demons in him.

If you have ever witnessed someone who is obviously demon possessed, you may have noticed that demons have distinct personalities. The possessed individual begins to manifest the personality of the demon possessing him.

A feminine-like spirit will sometimes speak in a soft, feminine voice out of a man's body. Or, conversely, a masculine-like spirit will sometimes speak in a manly voice out of a woman's body. It is not unusual for the possessed person to lose his or her identity to the demon within.

Antisocial Characteristics

Another thing I noticed about the people who are tormented by demons is a strong *tendency to shun other people.* The evil spirits in them usually cause them to be antisocial in their attitudes and behavior.

For example, in the fifth chapter of Mark, we find that the demoniac stayed away from other people. Not wanting to be with anyone, he lived alone, in the solitude of the tombs. This pathetic soul was obviously antisocial in his conduct.

I asked Jesus why this pattern held true so often, and He replied, "Satan doesn't like the people he possesses to fellowship with others, especially with those who are believers, because they might gain the knowledge to fight back."

Spiritually Insightful

While Jesus was showing me how evil spirits torment people, I also observed that a possessed person usually displayed a *marked degree of spiritual insight.*

Demons always recognized Jesus, sometimes before believers did. When Jesus was on earth, the unclean spirits He confronted often spoke out that they knew He was the Son of God, acknowledging His deity and ultimate power.

Jesus told me that demons always recognize God's servants, too, when they have the faith to exercise authority over them.

A miserable, unfortunate demoniac asked the Lord, *"Have You come here to torment us before the time?"* (Matthew 8:29 NKJV). The fact that the demons knew about impending judgment awaiting them in a future time shows remarkable spiritual insight.

Superhuman Strength

I saw demon-possessed persons who exhibited *superhuman strength*. No one was strong enough to subdue the demoniac of Gadara. When they tried to tie him up with chains and shackles, he would break them apart easily. He was uncontrollable and could not be confined. (See Mark 5:1–4.)

In my visions I saw many pathetic people bound by evil spirits. The striking thing I noticed about them was that they were always tormented. The awful price of giving oneself over to a demon is high.

The torment that accompanies demon possession is constant and without letup. Victims have no personal peace and get no real rest. They can also make it impossible for those nearby to have any peace, too.

Self-Destructive Tendencies

Another characteristic of a demon-possessed person is a *tendency toward self-destruction*. The demons that controlled the man from Gadara would eventually have destroyed him just as surely as they destroyed the swine they entered into. The man repeatedly cut himself with stones. (See Mark 5:5.) This self-mutilation is a pronounced form of self-destructive behavior that people in their right minds would never do.

The demon that possessed a boy in Mark 9 also showed these same signs of self-destruction that would eventually have killed him if Jesus had not cast out the demon and set the boy free.

A minister gave the following inspiring testimony of deliverance from demon possession that illustrates the power of God to set the captives free:

SETTING THE CAPTIVE FREE

As I entered the auditorium where I was to preach, a young man approached me. This young man had heard of the many who were being liberated in the meeting and had come because he, too, was bound.

The horrible demons of lust and perversion had possessed him as long as he could remember. The way those demons manifest themselves is described in the Word of God in this way:

> 27 And likewise also the men, leaving the natural use of the woman, burned in their lust one toward another; men with men working that which is unseemly. (Romans 1:27)

This man, who was in his early twenties, confessed that this horrible demon of homosexuality had controlled his life since he was a small boy.

He had been raised in a Christian home where family devotions were a daily practice. He had always prayed, as far back as he could remember. This young man had sought God for salvation many times. Many times the people who prayed for and with him urged him to "accept his salvation by faith."

However, he realized that he had never really been loosed or set free from the evil force that was within him. Although he would often go to the altar, where he would confess, repent, and "by faith" claim salvation, deep down within him something would never let loose. It was this demon of lust.

Frustrated by Bondage

He confessed to me: "I've tried so many times and failed, that now, no one, not even the pastor here, has any confidence in me or my desire to live for God. They say I don't really mean business with God, but I do. Every time there is a revival close by, I attend. And I go to the altar, because I want to stop committing this binding sin and live for God.

"Every time I go to the altar for salvation, the personal workers always tell me to 'take it by faith!' I tell them I know that deep down within me there is something that has never come out. I try to take it by faith, but soon I am right back doing the thing that I promised God I'd never do again!

"This is more than a mere temptation. It is an overwhelming, compelling, powerful force, from which it seems my prayers alone cannot free me. I believe the thing is a demon. If I can ever be loosed from this awful creature, I will show the people that I can live for God."

The "Thing" Is a Demon

I told the man to meet me at the altar call that night, and I would cast the demon out if he really wanted to be free from it!

Sometimes people ask me, "Isn't it enough just to preach the Word?"

Let me remind you that Christ did more than preach the Word! He set the captive free! He cast out devils! If just preaching the Word were sufficient, why didn't Jesus stop after He had given the people the Word?

When Christ gave the Great Commission, He told His disciples to do more than just preach the Word! He said to them, *"As ye go, preach....Heal the sick ...cast out devils"* (Matthew 10:7–8).

The young man I am telling you about had heard the Word preached all his life. He had prayed much himself. He had repented. He had "received his salvation by faith," according to his own testimony. But he had never really been born again. He had not experienced the miracle that made him know that his old life had passed away, as Scripture states:

> [17] Therefore, if anyone is in Christ, he is a new creation; old things have passed away; behold, all things have become new.
>
> (2 Corinthians 5:17 NKJV)

It is my conviction that in some cases, such as the demoniac at Gadara, a person must be loosed from demon power before he will ever be found *"sit-ting at the feet of Jesus, clothed, and in his right mind"* (Luke 8:35). The first thing Jesus did for the demoniac was to loose him from demon power!

After I had preached, I met the young man at the altar. He knelt and began to pray and seek God. I went to where he was praying, and as I stood by his side, I laid my hands upon him.

I intended to command the demon to come out of him, but as I touched him, he fell prostrate on the floor, completely overcome and unable to rise. A group of spiritually mature men joined me.

I knelt over him and began to pray and rebuke the demon forces. Suddenly, as I prayed, the young man began to choke. He clutched his throat with his hands and, looking up at me, said, "If you keep praying like that, I'll choke to death right here."

God revealed to me in that moment that it was the demon influencing the man to say these things. He wanted me to stop praying.

As I started to pray in earnest again, the evil spirit again started to come out.

But the man gagged, and began to choke again. Looking up at me, he cried out, "Please stop! If you continue to pray, I am going to die right here!"

I told the man that he wasn't going to die. He was going to live! He was going to be free!

A Filthy-Looking Mass

Again, I began to pray. I commanded the foul spirit to come out. At the same time the man began to choke. Then he began to vomit.

As I turned the man over on his side, one of the elders quickly spread out his handkerchief to receive the horrible thing that the young man was vomiting up. Many were horrified as they looked at the fleshy looking mass.

While the elder disposed of the handkerchief and its contents, the young man sat up, and the glory of God shone on his face. With a smile on his lips, he began to shout, "It's gone! Thank God, it is gone! I felt it leave! It just let loose, and it came out! For the first time I can remember, I am free from the thing!"

And to prove it, he has lived a victorious life and has proved to the people that he could live for God!

THE MIRACLE OF DELIVERANCE

Listen, my friend. This is a genuine miracle. It is a testimony of what God's power can do!

I was still in awe at all the wondrous things God was showing me.

Jesus spoke to me in an urgent tone. He told me to write down what I saw and to tell my readers that when people indulge in evil practices too long, they become trapped by a diabolical force that seeks to destroy them.

Many times the victim is placed in a bondage from which he or she cannot escape through mere human power. There are bondages that cannot be overcome by exercising the human will. Yet, Jesus declared repeatedly that anyone can be liberated from all of the devil's bondage. He affirmed to me that no demon is greater than the power of God.

He said that His power is available to all who believe His promises and obey

His Word, as it is recorded: *"Behold, I give you the authority...over all the power of the enemy"* (Luke 10:19 NKJV).

In the sixth chapter of Ephesians, Paul indicated that our warfare is not against flesh and blood. Rather, it is along spiritual lines. And in his second letter to the Corinthians, he said this:

> ³ For though we walk in the flesh, we do not war according to the flesh.
>
> ⁴ For the weapons of our warfare are not carnal but mighty in God for pulling down strongholds.
>
> (2 Corinthians 10:3–4 NKJV)

We are warring against evil authorities and powers in high places. We have the capability, through Jesus Christ and the power of the Holy Spirit, to bring them under control in our own lives.

But we can do this only as we reckon ourselves *"to be dead indeed unto sin, but alive unto God through Jesus Christ our Lord"* (Romans 6:11).

If you feel that you are bound by an evil spirit or by one of Satan's demons, remember as you read these words: God has greater power than the devil or his demons.

Jesus came to set you free! In Jesus' name, you will be free! Call on Him, our Master, now. Be determined to be free.

I urge you to follow the instructions found in God's Word and to take the actions suggested throughout this book.

God is sending His Spirit to you right now. *You will be free*, in Jesus' name!

Chapter 7

The Fight in the Garden

During all of these revelations of the spirit world, one truth that the Lord told me began to stand out in my mind: Demonic spirits cannot force their way into a human being's life without cooperation or submission on the individual's part. Jesus told me that demons cannot just overpower a person and take possession, although they long to do so.

What the evil spirits must do is to deceive us. They must find a way to trick us into yielding our wills to their influence and power.

When individuals voluntarily pay attention to the voice of the devil, then demons move in. They possess the mind. They control the thoughts. They end up dominating the entirety of the lives of their victims.

Jesus showed me that this was true from the beginning. The large number of angels who fell with Lucifer were not blatantly dominated by him and forced to yield. Instead, they were seduced and deceived. They willingly chose to follow him and obey his directives. Lucifer's seduction was subtle, but effective.

I began to understand that when Satan and his army fell from grace, they did not receive their final judgment, even though they suffered some immediate consequences. My Lord revealed to me that when Satan and his followers were kicked out of heaven (see Revelation 12:9), sentence was passed on them immediately. And the judgment of God continues to rest on them.

However, after Satan was changed from Lucifer into Satan, he still had access to God, as can be seen in the first chapter of Job. Even now, he is *"the prince of the power of the air"* (Ephesians 2:2).

But their final, eternal judgment is described in the Word as a lake of *"everlasting fire, prepared for the devil and his angels"* (Matthew 25:41), which is yet to be experienced. Sadly, all who reject Jesus and the sacrifice of the Father's love are condemned to go there, too.

Our Savior brought to my mind what he showed John on the isle of Patmos. After the fury of God's wrath is poured out on a corrupted earth during the Great Tribulation,

> [10] The devil that deceived them [will be] cast into the lake of fire and brimstone...and shall be tormented day and night.   (Revelation 20:10)

THE GARDEN CONFLICT AND ITS RESULTS

The Lord also reminded me that when Satan enticed Eve in the Garden of Eden, Adam and Eve both made a tragic, but deliberate, choice to sin against God. Although sentence was passed on the first couple immediately, they did not suffer instantaneous judgment and physical death until much later.

They did die spiritually that day, and they brought sin and physical death to the human family. But both Adam and Eve lived many years after this tragedy (Adam lived 930 years, according to Genesis 5:5), and they bore children together.

Just as God ejected Satan from the original paradise, so God drove Adam and Eve from their home in the Garden of Eden. Just as Satan's rebellion and fall plunged the universe into darkness, so Adam and Eve's sin brought terrible consequences to the earth.

Jesus explained to me that the present universe (the biblical "heavens and earth") is tainted with evil, and will ultimately be burned up and replaced with new heavens and a new earth.

> [10] But the day of the Lord will come as a thief in the night; in the which the heavens shall pass away with a great noise, and the elements shall melt with fervent heat, the earth also and the works that are therein shall be burned up.
>
> [11] Seeing then that all these things shall be dissolved, what manner of persons ought ye to be in all holy

conversation and godliness.

12 Looking for and hasting unto the coming of the day of God, wherein the heavens being on fire shall be dissolved, and the elements shall melt with fervent heat?

13 Nevertheless we, according to his promise, look for new heavens and a new earth, wherein dwelleth righteousness. (2 Peter 3:10-13)

The Lord showed me that at that point all wickedness and imperfection will be removed forever. Believers who have been faithful to God will live in His perfect new universe.

The universe will then be harmonious and complete. It will never again see corruption. Things will be as God originally intended them to be, only better. At last we will live in a universe without the possibility of evil.

UNTIL THEN

But we live on earth now, and until that day when our blessed Lord comes to take us home, we are engaged in spiritual warfare with Satan and his army.

Jesus showed me that the fight that is now in progress on the battlegrounds of our lives is the same fight with Satan that began in the Garden of Eden. The enemy is still subtle. He still deceives many.

To be victorious, born-again believers must put on the whole armor of God and be very alert and diligent in the fight against spiritual foes.

THE INVISIBLE BATTLE FOR HEALING

Once I was praying for a person in the hospital who had been very ill with a high fever for several days. God gave me a vision and showed me just how the spiritual battle over this particular sickness was taking place. He pulled back the curtains, at it were, and let me see exactly how the spiritual battle for healing was being fought.

I first saw the hospital building and then the room where this person lay suffering. There was a large window beside the bed.

Outside the window I saw a very large dragon. Its body was shaped like a classic dragon of medieval literature, but its hide was smooth instead of scaly.

As I looked out the window from my vantage point in the hospital room, I saw the threatening beast. It started coming toward us, but I wasn't alarmed because we were inside the building. It got closer and closer, and larger and larger.

Then I watched in fascination and horror as this fire-breathing monster forced its head through the large window. I saw it clamp its crushing teeth onto the sick person's neck.

The patient could not see the dragon, however. The nurses and the other people in the room could not see the dragon. But God allowed me to observe the actual spiritual conflict that was taking place.

Very quickly, the patient began to get worse. The young man's feverish body was cooking from a very high temperature. The nurses packed ice around him and tried to keep his temperature down that way.

They were doing all they could do, but their efforts were not helping. I cried out to God for this young man.

The Lord said to me: "Look, and listen to My instructions. Fight the real enemy, because you *'wrestle not against flesh and blood, but against principalities, against powers, against the rulers of the darkness of this world, against spiritual wickedness in high places'"* (Ephesians 6:12.)

"Dear God," I pleaded, "I know that my life is right before You. Teach me how to pray effectively. For in the name of Jesus, I know that Satan must flee!"

Keys to the Kingdom

The Lord began speaking to my spirit. He told me to take the keys to the kingdom and use them for His glory. He said that whatever I would bind on earth would be bound in heaven.

Suddenly I began to speak out with a powerful anointing: "I bind this devil with the Word of God! In Jesus' name this evil force must turn this young man loose."

I commanded the evil dragon to remove himself from the patient in Jesus' name and in accordance with the Word of God. Boldly, I spoke out, "In Jesus' name and by the blood that He shed, this young man *will* be healed and delivered!"

Hebrews 10:19 says that the blood of Jesus gives us boldness to enter the holiest of all holy places in earnest prayer and to have our petitions answered.

Angelic Assistance

Then I saw a new scenario. My eyes were drawn to the activity that was taking place in the heavenly realms.

I watched as a large, powerful angel came down from heaven with a mighty sword. He carried the Word of God and held it open. The large book was full of light and great power.

Then I saw this mighty angel bind the dragon that had its grip on the young man with such a high fever. The angel pulled the dragon away from him in Jesus' name. Fire flashed from the angel's sword, burning the evil spirit and causing it much agony.

As the warfare raged, I saw more angels of God help to bind the evil dragon with chains and drag it off to an arid place. (See Matthew 12:43 and Luke 11:24.)

The sick man who was on the hospital bed was set free. It was not a gradual healing. His fever broke immediately, and he was well. The doctors could not find out what caused the sickness or the sudden recovery.

AMAZING ACTIVITIES

The Lord showed me that it is the evil kingdom's delight to smash, to mangle, to twist, to mutilate, to disfigure, and to darken every shred of truth and every child of God in every way possible.

The aim of the devil is to distort. It makes no difference whether the affected objects are bodies or souls, flesh or ideas, matter or spirits. His negative powers are always used in destructive ways.

The great deceiver cannot create. He cannot make anything. Consequently, he can add nothing positive to human life.

The activities of Satan's army that I witnessed taking place amazed me. I saw demons of child molestation and demons of child abuse. Believe me, there are a lot of them.

I watched these demons talking to any person who would listen to them and give themselves over to them. The evil spirits showed those who were receptive to their ideas how to use all kinds of facades to hide their sinful, pernicious ways and deadly deeds.

Some of the demons that I saw were given special assignments to go to rock bands and singing groups and entertainers of the world. They would lead these influential, notorious performers into outlandish behavior and provoke them to engage unashamedly in sexual sins, the more perverted the better.

I saw a very large demon unit—a type of military division—that was engaged in persuading people to act out their inner lusts and desires. They would persuade anyone who would listen to explore all kinds of sins with great enthusiasm.

I saw demonic beings being assigned to blend ceremonial magic, sexual perversion, animal sacrifice, and illegal drugs into a powerful potion that lured people into engaging in sexual orgies that blasphemed God.

Periodically, a shout would arise from these evil spirits where a great number of them had gathered. I watched and listened and saw that they were celebrating the occasion of a group of people being won over to satanism.

I saw unclean spirits rejoicing that they could get people to worship the one they called their "exalted leader."

Demonic forces were being deployed everywhere in our culture, I noticed. They infiltrated every segment of society, both secular and religious. Although their warfare took many different forms, their single purpose, always, was to destroy the works of God.

Listen, my friend. These lying, deceiving spirits are after you and your walk with God. They are after your family and your relationships with others.

They will attack you through your emotions and through your circumstances. Because they are spirits, they never sleep.

Those who lightly dismiss the spiritual struggle are setting themselves up for disaster. The battle is real and personal. Only in the strength of Christ can we conquer.

How to Counterattack

We cannot win the battle in our own strength because we are overmatched. Jesus told me to tell people that they cannot win the battle with the world, the flesh, and the devil if they have sin in their lives. Many times in my own ministry, I have seen people try in vain to pray when they had sin in their lives. Sin always hinders our prayers because it keeps us out of close relationship with God.

The devil and his forces are crafty, cunning, deceitful, tricky, and cruel. You and I must wear spiritual armor if we are to defeat him.

> [11] Put on the whole armour of God, that ye may be able to stand against the wiles of the devil.
>
> [Ephesians 6:11]

Remember: Jesus and the Holy Spirit are more than a match for the enemy.

Chapter 8

A Tangible Terror

Oh, my friends, you can't imagine what sorrow and anger and fear seize people who give themselves to the evil one!

I saw Satan's hordes literally destroying lives. I watched in horror as they dragged people into the streets, making fools out of them in front of others. I saw individuals sell their souls without regard to the personal price they were paying.

It made me sick to see evil spirits turn their victims into unrecognizable, dirty, absurdly gullible pawns with no purpose or harmony in their lives.

Demons are real. They are more powerful than you could ever imagine.

Once I saw a horde of them traveling through the heavenlies to a particular location on earth. The swarm looked like a great black cloud that was ready to storm but somehow couldn't.

I saw evil spirits hovering over individuals, trying to make them nervous. Their presence and their torment seemed like a tangible terror.

THE DEMON OF FEAR

I stood with the blessed Lord Jesus in what I can only describe as a celestial viewing balcony. We could see all the way into heaven. We could see things happening on the earth. And we could see the spiritual underground with all of its hellishness.

Spirit beings, invisible to the flesh, were visible to my eyes. A parade of activities from the spiritual underworld passed before us in panoramic view.

Below me I watched an ugly demon of fear attack a well-dressed business-woman. She began to see darkness and evil in ordinary, mundane things. She grew edgier and jumpier. As time passed, she turned into a tense, white-knuckled "basket case," living in continual dread and confusion.

When she was alone, she often whimpered like a child trying to be silent. She paced the floor. She began to let out blood-curdling screams.

Fear kept her stomach tied in knots. She often felt like she was about to explode from a pressure that kept building deep within her being. She would become frantic when she actually took the time to think about what she could do.

Listen, friend, you don't have to look under your bed to find an evil spirit of fear. You don't have to wait for one to hunt you down. They can find you wherever you are if you let your guard down. Hell's emissaries knock at every person's door. And they don't need keys to come into your house if you leave the tiniest crack open for them.

I saw those foul spirits of fear, those fiends from hell, gradually fill the minds of individuals with scary visions of nightmare shapes. These imaginary monsters would reach out in the darkness to claw, bite, and scream at the victim.

I heard one of these spirits of fear wooing a victim. It said to a poor, unsuspecting soul: "I know you. I perceive much in your character that pleases me. You have an inner strength that others don't have. You have a strength of courage and willpower that is uncommon among other mortals. You will go far if you will go with me."

I saw another woman who was possessed by a demon of claustrophobia, which is the fear of being closed in or of being confined in tight spaces. She said that she was never able to breathe freely in a small room, especially if it had no windows.

In addition, she always felt cold. On the hottest day she felt a numbing chill clinging to her like a shroud.

All day and especially at night she could hear lonely, mournful sounds humming in her subconscious. The darkness that surrounded her filled her like an abyss. Fearful visions of nightmare shapes haunted her mind.

She regressed at a steady pace until she lost all sense of time and space. The telltale effects of demon possession on a victim are horrid beyond words.

Again, the Scriptures corroborate the awful things I am describing to you. Jesus met many people afflicted by demons:

> 24 Then His fame went throughout all Syria; and they brought to Him all sick people who were afflicted with various diseases and torments, and those who were demon-possessed, epileptics, and paralytics; and He healed them.
>
> (Matthew 4:24 NKJV)

PAINFUL POSSESSION

Great torment was the most common characteristic of all the people I saw who were occupied or controlled by evil spirits. All of them were tortured souls; they all suffered much pain.

The Bible points out that when a demon overtakes a person, the individual won't get any better unless the demon is cast out.

X   In fact, the Bible says that as we near the end of the age, demon activity will increase. John saw this phenomenon in stark pictures:

> [13] Then I saw three evil spirits that looked like frogs; they came out of the mouth of the dragon, out of the mouth of the beast and out of the mouth of the false prophet.
>
> [14] They are spirits of demons performing miraculous signs, and they go out to the kings of the whole world, to gather them for the battle on the great day of God Almighty.
>
> (Revelation 16:13–14 NIV)

Victims of demon possession often had broken and bruised bodies. They had hideous spiritual and emotional injuries, but they were maimed physically as well. This is biblically verified, as we read in Luke:

> [39] And behold, a spirit seizes him, and he suddenly cries out; it convulses him so that he foams at the mouth, and it departs from him with great difficulty, bruising him.
>
> (Luke 9:39 NKJV)

Evil spirits break the body. Some demon-possessed people I saw were very emaciated and looked almost like skeletons. Demon spirits in a person cause his body to dry up and wither away.

I saw unclean spirits go into human bodies, making them unhealthy and causing severe physical problems. They can cause severe psychological and emotional problems. An evil spirit can break a person's spirit.

> [22] A merry heart doeth good like a medicine: but a broken spirit drieth the bones. (Proverbs 17:22)

I saw many peculiar behaviors of people who were possessed by devils. The Bible tells of a boy who was possessed by a demon and delivered by Jesus. The boy's father described his behavior this way when he took his son to Jesus:

> [15] "Lord, have mercy on my son," he said. "He has seizures and is suffering greatly. He often falls into the fire or into the water." (Matthew 17:15 NIV)

And here is Luke's complete account of that event:

> [38] Suddenly a man from the multitude cried out, saying, "Teacher, I implore You, look on my son, for he is my only child.
>
> [39] "And behold, a spirit seizes him, and he suddenly cries out; it convulses him so that he foams at the mouth, and it departs from him with great difficulty, bruising him.
>
> [40] "So I implored Your disciples to cast it out, but they could not."
>
> [41] Then Jesus answered and said, "O faithless and perverse generation, how long shall I be with you and bear with you? Bring your son here."
>
> [42] And as he was still coming, the demon threw him down and convulsed him. Then Jesus rebuked the unclean spirit, healed the child, and gave him back to his father.
>
> (Luke 9:38–42 NKJV)

I saw some people who suffered great injury and pain, just like that boy did, because they were thrown around by the evil spirits that possessed them. At first,

I was stunned when I saw demons throw their victims down in a violent way! But then, Jesus reminded me that Satan's ultimate aim was and is to harm and destroy life, no matter how nice it may look to begin with.

HOW MANY DEMONS?

Unlimited numbers of demons can possess an unsaved person.

When Jesus rose from the dead, the first person He revealed Himself to was *"Mary Magdalene, out of whom he had cast seven devils"* (Mark 16:9).

In Mark 5:9, a possessed man had a *"Legion"* of demons in him. A legion was the main division of troops in the Roman army. The number of soldiers in a legion varied at different periods from about 3,000 to 6,000 soldiers. We know there were a minimum of about 2,000 demons in the man because that many hogs were destroyed in the sea when the evil spirits were sent into the swine.

I saw the many millions of dirty, filthy spirits of darkness gradually dragging down those whom they possessed.

Life for their victims always grew progressively worse. Little by little the evil spirit would get the person to yield more authority until the victim was obeying the demon without question. The person seemed to be under a spell.

Jesus delivered a man from demons who had begun living in a cemetery, *"among the tombs"* (Mark 5:3). Perhaps the demons persuaded the man to dwell there in order to make life more uncomfortable for him. Or maybe it was to make him appear wild and menacing in order to scare others away. At any rate, the demons made him unfit to live in decent society:

> ³ This man lived in the tombs, and no one could bind him any more, not even with a chain.
>
> ⁴ For he had often been chained hand and foot, but he tore the chains apart and broke the irons on his feet. No one was strong enough to subdue him.
>
> ⁵ Night and day among the tombs and in the hills he would cry out and cut himself with stones.
>
> (Mark 5:3–5 NIV)

However, those malicious, malignant, filthy creatures from hell had to vacate the man's body when Jesus took authority over them.

[8] For Jesus had said to him, "Come out of this man, you evil spirit!"

[9] Then Jesus asked him, "What is your name?" "My name is Legion," he replied, "for we are many."

[10] And he begged Jesus again and again not to send them out of the area.

[11] A large herd of pigs was feeding on the nearby hillside.

[12] The demons begged Jesus, "Send us among the pigs; allow us to go into them."

[13] He gave them permission, and the evil spirits came out and went into the pigs. The herd, about two thousand in number, rushed down the steep bank into the lake and were drowned.

[14] Those tending the pigs ran off and reported this in the town and countryside, and the people went out to see what had happened.

[15] When they came to Jesus, they saw the man who had been possessed by the legion of demons,

> sitting there, dressed and in his right mind; and they were afraid.
>
> (Mark 5:8–15 NIV)

I saw demons and evil spirits controlling, harassing, and tormenting individuals. I saw them driving a person to do things he ought not to do, and to do things he wished he had not done.

Using uncontrolled tempers, unmanageable depression, unreal fears, suicidal thoughts, psychosomatic sicknesses, and feelings of total rejection, evil spirits tormented a man until he broke completely.

A demon of suicide entered into one man I saw, and shortly after that he took his own life.

As demons entered into a woman, I could see them infiltrating her entire being. Once they had taken up residence in her body, she began to have frequent bouts with all kinds of sicknesses.

Foul spirits occupied her mind and controlled her emotions. They manipulated her will. They caused her to think, do, and act in ways she did not really want to.

DESTRUCTIVE DEMONS

✓ It was obvious to me that some of the evil spirits caused men and women to murder and maim each other. I watched them cunningly motivate individuals to act violently and irrationally. These people who were being possessed lived only to inflict excruciating pain and suffering on other people.

Some of the evil spirits I saw were at work in other areas of people's lives. Some did not appear to be as violent as others seemed to be.

I saw spirits of thievery enter into many people, causing them to live lives of deceit. They began to steal and to cheat. Some became compulsive thieves, or kleptomaniacs.

Some people yielded to Satan and were possessed by lying demons. They became compulsive liars. Others merely had a spirit of lying: they exercised their evil gift by misrepresenting everything and would exaggerate without having any apparent reason to do so.

Those people who yielded their bodies to the destructive and mesmerizing lure of the deceitful fallen angels ultimately destroyed themselves.

HOPE IN THE MIDST

Before this seems bleak and hopeless, I must tell you that I saw angels overthrowing demons and driving out unclean spirits.

I saw Jesus casting the demons out of people with only a word! I saw Him command a demon of perversion to loose a young man who had become entangled with lust and homosexuality. The demons had to leave.

God's Word affirms this truth:

> [16] When evening had come, they brought to Him many who were demon-possessed. And He cast out the spirits with a word, and healed all who were sick.
>
> (Matthew 8:16 NKJV)

Jesus can cast out a demon with a word!

I saw a woman who could not talk because she had been demonized. A mute spirit had possessed her, and she could not communicate. When Jesus met a man who had a similar demon, He cast the foul spirit out:

> [32] As they went out, behold, they brought to Him a man, mute and demon-possessed.
>
> [33] And when the demon was cast out, the mute spoke. And the multitudes marveled, saying, "It was never seen like this in Israel!"
>
> [Matthew 9:32–33 NKJV]

"Demons cannot get into your spirit if you are a child of Mine," Jesus told me. "Your spirit is the real you. That is the place where I dwell within you. As long as I dwell there, a demon cannot cohabit with Me."

ANGELS ASSIST IN DELIVERANCE

Once God opened up the spirit world to me, and I saw angels everywhere. As Scripture was being spoken, the Word seemed to leap off the page of the Bible and take the form of a sword.

That awe-inspiring sword would pierce a person's body and go straight to his or her problem and heal the individual.

In my book *A Divine Revelation of Heaven,* I testify about what I saw in one of the visions God gave me:

> When it was time for the altar call, I saw angels going among the congregation, nudging people to go to the altar and give their hearts to the Lord. When I saw the angels touching the hearts of individuals, the blackest sins began to churn up and out of their hearts as they knelt and prayed to God. Oh, it was beautiful!
>
> In my spirit I could see chains that were wrapped around the people. As people received forgiveness, angels seemed to break the bondage, to shatter the chains, to cast them off. The bands broke as people began to raise their hands and confess their sins to the Lord.
>
> Cries and shouts went up everywhere from souls who had been delivered. It was wonderful.
>
> In many of my services all over the world, God has provided great miracles like these, with healing and deliverance happening.

I praise God for His signs, wonders, and miracles. I know that the angels are at work, helping me with the ministry of the Lord Jesus Christ.

Friend, as I mused over the many things He was showing me, I wept because I knew that the power of Christ is stronger than all of the powers of hell!

God's power is available for you now. If you are being tormented by evil spirits, you, too, can be delivered and set free from this tangible terror by which you are bound.

Chapter 9

Demons of Addiction

"Come with Me," Jesus said, and He took me on another revelatory journey across the ocean to a large city. Although I knew it was a foreign city, nevertheless, I heard people speaking in English, while the signs were in several languages.

As in the other revelations God gave to me, I could supernaturally see evil spirits and could hear what people were saying. The people could not see me or hear me, however.

I saw inside a nightclub in the downtown section of this large city. Demons were swarming like flies over the building, inside and outside the club.

The evil spirits appeared in all kinds of grotesque shapes and hideous forms. They all seemed to be having a grand time as they interacted with the clientele who patronized this den of iniquity.

A TRIP INTO HELL

As I looked, my eyes began to focus on a young man who was strung out on drugs. Suddenly, I realized that the young man could see the demons, too. He began to scream as loudly as he could, "Help me, please! I am caught in the fires of hell! I am burning up!"

Someone quickly stepped to the terrified youth's side and asked him if everything was all right.

"All right? Heavens, no! What are they doing here?" He pointed to some nearby demons that his friend could not see. "Don't you see those demons? Can't you feel those infernal flames?"

The friend began talking to the fearful young man in a clear, distinct voice. I recognized that this friend was a Christian. Jesus told me that he was there that night to witness for the Lord.

Realizing the spiritual implications of what was taking place, the Christian was filled with Christ's compassion for this lost soul. I watched as he gently used the Scriptures and began to lead the drugged-out youth to the Savior.

"God is here!" the believer insisted. "He is everywhere, even here in this place. But you have to choose between God and the devil."

A few minutes later when the drug-induced fog began to lift from his mind, this user screamed at the top of his lungs, "I CHOOSE GOD!"

Saints, when he said that, I could see the demons scatter in all directions! They fled from the young man as fast as they could.

They seemed to recognize the determination of the youth and the decision he was making, and they left him alone. The young man knelt in the glare of the neon lights with that Christian friend, prayed the sinner's prayer, and gave his heart to Christ.

At that moment when he decided to give his life to God, the young man was freed from his addictions.

A Cloud of Addictions

By far, the spirits of addiction are the most numerous of all the demonic types in the dark underworld.

Jesus showed me the entire globe, and I saw a blue haze surrounding this world. At first I thought, "How beautiful!"

Then Jesus corrected me: "What you see is not the natural air. It is an atmosphere of addiction that covers the whole earth. People are becoming addicted to all kind of substitutes that cause pain and suffering beyond measure."

I saw the many, many spirits of addiction and observed the way they operated.

A marijuana demon slipped a smooth rope around a beautiful young woman. At first the rope felt good to her. But the demon tightened the rope just a little. When she took another hit, he tightened the rope a little more. After a little while, I noticed that the smooth rope had turned into a chain.

Still, she could easily slip the chain on or off at this point. But as time passed, the chain got tighter and tighter.

Finally, she could no longer take it off, and she was bound.

The demon that did this to her wooed her and cajoled her, while all the time it was binding her and chaining her. Then the monster began tormenting her mercilessly.

TESTIMONIES FROM FORMER ADDICTS

Jesus told me to describe addiction in such a way that gives hope for the sufferer. Perhaps the best way I can do that and describe the work of these evil fiends of addiction is to relate some testimonies of people who have been delivered by the power of God. Every single one of these testimonies is real. Here are some personal stories from those who have gone down that long road of addiction.

Looking for Love in All the Wrong Places

For fifteen years I was addicted to drugs and alcohol. I was a prostitute, a thief, and a liar. I was drunk or stoned every night.

I would do anything to support my habit. I did not "decide" one day that I would become a prostitute, any more than I chose to become a drug user and an alcoholic. They were just things I started doing to try to fill the hurt places inside.

I was searching for acceptance and love from friends and loved ones. I wanted acceptance from society, but found none. I thought I had to have sex to receive love.

My addiction cost me everything that was of any value to me. I lost my home, my job, my family, my health, and my self-respect.

I was beaten, raped, robbed, and left with nothing. My life was spared only because God had a plan for me.

Thank God, He has delivered me from my addictions. For the past three years I have been living a clean life without any drugs, alcohol, cigarettes, or other harmful chemicals.

The Lord has restored to me everything that the devil took away. He has blessed me beyond measure. Since He has saved me and delivered me, I just praise Jesus for freedom from the devil's addictions.

The Adult Thing to Do

When I was a young child, my unwed mother was never home, and I was left with all kinds of people to take care of me. I was easy prey for sexual abuse.

At thirteen I married a man who began physically abusing me almost from the beginning. I became a mother at fourteen, and started drinking and smoking pot because I thought that was the "adult" thing to do. I thought that since I had a baby, I must be an adult!

I partied, drank, smoked, stole, and had no love for myself or any self-respect. I became snared more and more. Things only got worse. I slipped deeper into hard drugs. I used cocaine, tequila, quaaludes, and angel dust.

Eight years ago God led me to a small church where He delivered me from my habits and used some caring people to love me back to respectability.

Thank God, He makes me higher than any drug or shot of gin ever did!

Raised in the Church

I was raised in church. I was there every Sunday morning, Sunday night, and Wednesday night. As a child, I went forward to accept Christ as my personal Savior.

As an adult, however, I slipped and got into drugs. Not only did I use and abuse them, I sold them. When I awoke in the hospital with yellow eyes and yellow skin, I was informed that my liver had swollen to four times its normal size. Suddenly I realized that I had reached the end of the line.

Praise God, He had someone there at that time to talk to me and to lead me back to Christ. Now, I am free of addiction and have a healthy liver. *"For with God nothing shall be impossible"* (Luke 1:37).

On a Treadmill to Hell

I began using drugs at the age of sixteen. I started out smoking marijuana, and I was an avid drinker by the time I was nineteen.

I began experimenting with snorting cocaine when I was twenty. By the time I was twenty-three, my world had begun to fall apart. But the day I was introduced to crack cocaine began ten long years of a hard and miserable life.

During my fight with the addiction monster, I was raped, beaten, and shot at. I was pistol-whipped and raped by three men once. I have had guns put to my head more than once.

I was so wrapped up in my addiction that I didn't want anyone to stop me. I was destroying the life that God had given me, but I just wanted to be left alone.

One night I was on my way to get high with another drug user when Jesus stopped me in my tracks and sent me back home. I realized that the God my mother had told me about all my life was arresting me just like He did Saul on the way to Damascus. (See Acts 9:1–6.)

He took the desire to do drugs, to drink, and to hang out with my former friends completely away from me. I am now delivered from that cold, dark life of despair and pain and suffering.

"If you...believe in your heart...you will be saved" (Romans 10:9 NKJV).

From Trauma in Childhood

I was sexually molested from the time I was three. In the second grade I started having homosexual feelings, and since then I've struggled with lesbian desires and thoughts.

At times I would feel as if I was totally insane. My head told me that it was okay to have these feelings, but in my heart I knew God was telling me to draw near to Him.

In college, I realized I was in bondage to the enemy and that only Christ could free me. Thank God, He did! I now have a wonderful life with a Christian husband who understands where I have come from.

Changed Only by God

At the age of four, I was raped by two men. This abuse continued until I was thinking, dreaming, and practicing homosexuality. I liked it, and I felt loved because I thought my abusers were beautiful men.

Eventually, I began to go from lover to lover. At first I thought they loved me. Soon I began selling my body to older and younger men, and I began to hate myself.

I hated the world and what it was doing to me. I got into drugs and drinking. Finally I was raped, stabbed, and left on the street for dead.

In the hospital a Christian nurse led me to Christ and showed me what the love of Jesus is for the first time.

The Lord set me free from the perversion and replaced it with His love. I am now married, and God has given us two wonderful children.

Power to Break an Addiction

I was a normal weed-smoking punk gangster and alcoholic about a month ago. Yet, I was depressed about all the bad things I was doing. Then, God hit me full force with His Holy Spirit. The feeling was so amazing and powerful that I cried. I have quit smoking weed and getting drunk. *"I love the LORD because He has heard my voice"* (Psalm 116:1).

GOD'S MESSAGE TO ADDICTS

Friends, I have a special burden on my heart for the addict. It doesn't matter what your addiction is or how long it has bothered you.

Jesus has the power to set you free. And because you are reading this book, I know that you want to be free. I believe that Jesus has already begun the work to deliver you. Obey Him. Follow His instructions.

Call on the Lord now!

Chapter 10

A Strategy for Destruction

The Lord took me into the heaven-lies so that I could see a panoramic view of the entire universe. One of the scenes I saw in the many revelations of God concerning the spirit world was a graphic display of evil spirits oppressing people.

Invisible to the natural world, they hovered near a struggling saint of God waiting for a vulnerable moment in her life. Then they pounced on her, burdening her soul and oppressing her spirit.

I saw the life-draining load of the cares of life and the concerns of daily living crush the joy from this child of God. The spiritual underworld's opposition to her relationship with the Lord was grinding, pressing, and straining. It hindered her spiritual progress and handicapped her walk with God.

I saw many evil spirits of depression attacking God's people. I saw a demon of depression use all of its deceit and cunning to persuade a believer to compare himself with others around him who seemed to be prospering. As the believer began to look at others and take his eyes off Jesus, he began to sink in sadness and discouragement.

I watched in disgust as the evil spirit dragged him down to the very pits of despondency. I saw that evil, conniving spirit of darkness laugh with glee and dance up and down as it began to boast to its fellow imps that they would have this person yet.

Suddenly, I saw powerful beams of light flashing through space. My eyes followed the laser-like rays to the earth, and I saw intercessors praying for despondent Christians and for depressed believers.

As I watched in amazement, a different mighty beam emerged from each believer who was interceding. These rays burned through the ether of space. The beams went all the way to heaven to the very throne of God!

A CALL FROM GOD

Immediately I felt the Lord's anointing throughout my entire being. I perceived that the extraordinary things He was showing to me had a specific meaning. I knew He was showing them to me for a special purpose.

I am always conscious of the fact that God's revelations carry with them an awesome responsibility for me, but at that moment His vision was extremely powerful and almost overwhelming.

God placed His hand on me and conveyed this message to my heart:

> Kathryn, for this purpose you were born, to write and tell what I have shown you and told you. For these things are faithful and true.
>
> Your call is to let the world know that there is a heaven, that there is

a hell, and that I, Jesus, was sent by God to save them from torment and to prepare a place for them in heaven.

You must let the people know that the spiritual is more lasting and eternal than the physical.

RADIANT BEAMS OF LIGHT

The message of the mighty beams of light was a revelation about prayer. I could see angels in heaven waiting to receive the beams of light.

Then God showed me that the heavenly beams represented the prayers of believers that are offered in intercession. I saw angels in heaven record each prayer on a scroll, writing down what the individual on earth had prayed. They would take the prayers and present them to God.

GOD'S PROTECTIVE RESOURCES

In prayer and meditation on the Word, you can find God, and He will speak to you just as He speaks to me. He is always present. When you take the time to listen, you will hear Him as He speaks.

Many times I am compelled to stop the day's usual activities and to study the Scriptures and pray. And when I do, I feel very close to Him. I feel like a little child waiting to receive instructions from my Father.

God told me to write to you about my many revelations concerning the spiritual battles involved in praying and serving Him. He told me to tell you that interceding prayer is the key to unlocking the blessings of heaven. The power of intercession cannot be measured.

As you and I walk together, please open your heart to receive from the Lord Jesus everything He has for you. He will teach you how to pray and believe in Him. He will show you the tactics of the devil and his army, and He will show you how to win the victory.

As I have been writing this book, the power of God has been so real. I have seen the struggle that goes on between good and evil. Between God and Satan. Between demons and angels. Between unclean spirits and the Holy Spirit.

The struggles I have seen were more than just various battle scenes in the war of good and evil, however. The Almighty showed me what was really happening in the spiritual realm.

I have witnessed the behind-the-scenes events that explain perfectly what takes place in the spirit world when Christians go through a hard battle or a tough fight.

Here is my account of a revelation God gave me of a young man who found himself in the fight of his life:

ATTACKED BY DEMONS

I saw a high school student in his room listening to ungodly music. "This young man has been dabbling in cultic practices," Jesus said. "All his life he has been taught to do right, but lately he has been too careless. Behold, the works of evil."

As the teenager lay on his bed, absorbing the throbbing, pounding rhythm of the ungodly music, he looked up and saw a demon fly into the room. Suddenly, he was filled with fear.

When the demon passed through the wall, he felt a cold breeze sweep through the room. The boy reached over and switched off the radio. He began to shiver and reached for a blanket.

About that time, the demon knocked a picture of Jesus off the wall. To the terrified boy, it seemed to fall off the wall by itself.

Then the demon turned the bedside radio back on. The evil spirit was still invisible to the teenager, but he could feel its presence. He shrank back in horror.

Fear filled the room like a thick fog. The air was heavy, almost too thick to breathe or to move through.

"Who is it?" the boy managed to call out in a quaking voice. In his heart, however, he knew it was a spirit of evil. So the boy began to pray to the Lord to make the demon leave the house and to place His angels around the place.

As he called out to God, the radio switched off by itself. The air immediately went back to normal.

At that moment, the boy's Christian parents happened to be passing by the room when they heard the unusual noises. They knocked on the door and went in to find their son calling on God. Although they did not know what had just occurred in the room, they began to pray with their son.

As they prayed, the boy saw a huge warrior angel with a mighty sword come into the room and drive the evil spirit out. He began to thank the Lord for deliverance. He was saved from what would have turned into demonic possession.

> [36] What a word this is! For with authority and power He commands the unclean spirits, and they come out. (Luke 4:36 NKJV)

Here is an illustrative story that gives a glimpse into the twisted thinking of the evil one:

A TALE OF THREE FIENDS

One day the bad spirits met together and resolved that our human race was too happy. A delegation of infernals was sent to earth on a mission of mischief.

One spirit said, "I will take charge of the vineyards!" Another said, "I will look after the grain fields!" Another said, "I will take charge of the music!"

The first spirit entered the vineyard one bright morning and sat down on the twisted root of a grapevine in sheer discouragement. He could not at first plan any harm for the vineyard.

The clusters were so full and purple and luscious and pure. The air was fairly bewitched with their sweetness. Health seemed to breathe from every ripened bunch.

But in wrath at so much loveliness, the fiend grasped a cluster in his right hand and squeezed it with utter hate, and, lo, his hand was red with the liquid and began to smoke!

Then the fiend laughed and said gleefully, as he looked at the crimson stream dripping from his hand: "That makes me think of the blood of broken hearts. I will strip the vineyards of their fruit, squeeze out all the clusters, let the juices stand until they rot, and will call the process 'fermentation.'"

A great vat was made, and men seeing it, brought cups and pitchers and dipped them in. They went off, drinking as they went, until they dropped in long lines of death.

When the fiend of the vineyards wanted to go back to his home in the pit, he trod over the bodies of the slain all the way, going down a causeway of the dead.

The fiend of the grain field waded chin-deep through the barley and the rye. As he came in, he found all the grain talking about bread, and prosperous husbandmen, and thrifty homes.

But the fiend thrust his long arms through the barley and the rye, pulled them up and flung them into the water, and kindled fires beneath by a spark from his own heart. There came a grinding and a mashing and a stench.

And men dipped their bottles into the fiery juice and staggered and blasphemed and rioted and fought and murdered until the fiend from the grain field changed his residence from the pit to a whiskey barrel.

There he sits by the doorway, laughing merrily at the fact that out of so harmless a thing as barley and rye, he has made the world a pandemonium.

The fiend of music entered a local tavern and found only a few customers. So he made a circuit of the city and gathered up all the instruments of sweet sound.

After the night had fallen, he marshaled a band. The trombones blew and the cymbals clapped and the harp strummed and the drums beat and the bugle called, and the crowds thronged into the pub and listened.

With wine cups in their right hands, they began to whirl in a dance that grew wilder and stronger and rougher, until the room shook and the glasses cracked and the floor broke through and the crowd dropped into hell.

They had done their work so well, the fiends of the vineyards and grain fields and music, that, on getting back together, high carnival was held.

Satan announced from his throne that there was no danger of the earth's redemption as long as vineyards and orchards and grain fields and music paid such large homage to the diabolical.

Then all the devils and spirits and demons cried, "Hear ye! Hear ye!" Lifting up their chalices of fire, they drank a toast to the alcohol merchants who peddle a product that binds and destroys instead of blesses and uplifts.

A POWERFUL SPIRITUAL RESOURCE

Listen, friends; in my visions I have seen Satan, the monarch of all wickedness, sitting on a throne of power, receiving his emissaries from all over the world. He was supervising all kinds of evil mischief; and what he could not do himself, he assigned to others to do for him.

I realized that every human being has a besieging, malignant spirit dogging his or her footsteps, trying to make the person think or act wrongly.

Likewise, the Lord showed me that each person on earth has a good angel assigned as a guardian. Believers who fear God have a whole troop of angels encamped about them.

Just remember, child of God, His angels are only a prayer away! When you call on Jesus, He dispatches His supernatural angels to minister to you and to rescue you. God provides sufficient resources for every situation.

THE DAY THE WITCHES WENT TO CHURCH

In my ministry I have often seen the hand of God reveal the evil one and deliver those who are bound.

A few years ago, I went to Columbus, Ohio, to speak at a special meeting that was sponsored by a group of ten area churches. About 1,500 people were in the service that night, along with the pastors from the various sponsoring churches. It was a wonderful meeting with the presence of the Lord all around us.

As the service progressed, the singers sang and the sponsoring churches and pastors were introduced. Then the host pastor introduced me to speak on *A Divine Revelation of Hell.*

As I stepped up to the podium, I felt my throat trying to close up on me. At the pulpit, I reached for a glass of water. As I was taking a sip, the Holy Spirit prompted me to say, "All you witches can stand up." That startling statement was completely unrehearsed, and it certainly was not premeditated.

Immediately, five people in the congregation stood up. They seemed to just pop up out of their seats like human jack-in-the-boxes.

Then I told the five witches who were standing that they could get help through Jesus. When I said this, the deacons came to the front immediately, ready to be of service.

I told the five witches (two men and three women) who were standing, "These deacons are here to help you find your way, if you want help through Jesus."

Two of them left the service to find their own way that night. The other three went with the deacons to find their way to salvation through Jesus!

Rooms had been set aside for the purpose of prayer, and the deacons escorted the witches to these rooms. As they prayed together, a mighty work of the Lord fell on them.

Meanwhile, I began my testimony of *A Divine Revelation of Hell.* During my testimony I could hear cries of great sorrow coming from the prayer rooms.

Many people in the congregation began to pray as I continued to speak.

After a time the sounds of sorrow stopped and were replaced by screams and loud pounding noises from the prayer rooms.

The saints continued to intercede, and I continued to give my testimony.

After a short while, the sounds of screaming and pounding in the rooms changed to shouts of "JESUS! JESUS! JESUS!"

Within the next few minutes the Holy Spirit brought joy and happiness to everyone there. The three people were no longer witches. They had asked for salvation through Jesus Christ our Lord, and He had delivered them from out of that dark pit!

Friends, the delivering, healing, saving power of Jesus is awesome. And each of God's redeemed saints has more power available than is needed to defeat the devil and all of his cohorts!

Chapter 11

Angels, God's Secret Army

In another vision, a huge angel of the Lord came to me and said, "Behold the wonderful beauty and the glory of your God."

I was taken up instantly into the heavenlies and through the gates into heaven. Each gate in heaven was made of an exquisite pearl, with intricate designs in it. The beauty of heaven is stunning to behold!

We passed the River of Life, and I could hear people shouting and praising God. I was taken before the throne of God. Oh, what shouts and what worship!

Saints, I saw the throne of God just like Holy Scripture says. It has a rainbow around it. It is overshadowed with the cloud of glory and the brilliance of the power of God. I heard voices, saw lightning, and heard thunder. I saw the divine manifestations of the power of God!

> [2] Immediately I was in the spirit; and, behold, a throne was set in heaven, and one sat on the throne.
>
> [3] ...And there was a rainbow round about the throne, in sight like unto an emerald.
>
> [5] And out of the throne proceeded lightnings and thunderings and voices: and there were seven lamps of fire burning before the throne, which are the seven Spirits of God.
>
> (Revelation 4:2-3, 5)

ARMIES OF ANGELS

As I looked, I heard the multiplied millions of voices of angels around the throne. The number of them there was inestimable. In Revelation, John beautifully described the scene I saw:

[11] And I beheld, and I heard the voice of many angels round about the throne and the beasts and the elders: and the number of them was ten thousand times ten thousand, and thousands of thousands.

[12] Saying with a loud voice, Worthy is the Lamb that was slain to receive power, and riches, and wisdom, and strength, and honour, and glory, and blessing.

(Revelation 5:11–12)

[11] And all the angels stood round about the throne, and about the elders and the four beasts, and fell before the throne on their faces, and worshipped God.

(Revelation 7:11)

The angels I saw in heaven seemed to be very large, mighty beings! They wore glistening garments that radiated huge amounts of light. They were powerful and always seemed to be sincere and respectful. They had their minds set to obey God.

It became obvious to me that the mighty angels I saw at the gates of pearl in heaven were protecting angels. At the side of each of these protecting angels was a massive sword.

I thought, *Well, glory to God! Hallelujah! God surely protects His children.*

The angels I saw on earth did not all look the same. I pondered over this until I began to look at the appearance of angels in the Bible:

- 📖 In Genesis 18:2, angels appeared to Abraham looking like a man.
- 📖 In Zechariah 5:9, angels appeared as women with wind in their wings.
- 📖 Psalm 104:4 says that angels are spirits; therefore, they are usually invisible.
- 📖 Hebrews 13:2 says that angels can appear to us as strangers.

ANGELS THAT PROTECT

The main function of some of the angels I saw interacting with humans was to guard them and the things of God. They were always armed.

Their duties often seemed to involve guarding sacred things. They prevented humans from getting too close to them, and kept the devil and demons from causing havoc and confusion with the sacred things of God. For example, when God drove Adam and Eve from the Garden of Eden, He placed these protecting angels, cherubim, *"to guard the way to the tree of life"* (Genesis 3:24 NKJV).

Likewise, the presence of God dwelt *"between the cherubim"* (1 Samuel 4:4 NKJV), or the protecting angels that were over the ark of the covenant

I saw one of these protecting angels push a speeding automobile out of the way to keep it from crashing into and killing one of God's saints. I saw a protecting angel guide a child away from danger, and the child never realized what the danger was or what was happening in the spirit world. I watched a protecting angel pull the mighty, protecting sword from its side and drive away a demon that was attacking a child of God!

> [11] For he shall give his angels charge over thee, to keep thee in all thy ways.

¹² They shall bear thee up in their hands, lest thou dash thy foot against a stone. (Psalm 91:11-12)

ANGELS AND THE WORD

I saw other angels giving out the Word of God to different people at various times. The angels didn't preach the Word themselves, but they gave it to God's servants whose calling is to proclaim the Gospel.

At times they would furnish a special word for a special need. When a believer needed special help from the Word of God, they would provide total recall of the promises of God.

Then I remembered that the Bible says the law was *"ordained by angels"* (Galatians 3:19) and that the words spoken through angels will prove to be *"steadfast"* (Hebrews 2:2 NKJV).

Friends, Jesus told me to tell you not to worry because He will send angels to protect you in the times of trouble and to bring you strength and sustenance from the promises of God in times of need!

These angels seemed to be especially adept at helping to get the Word of God out to the lost, particularly by aiding the men and women of God whose responsibility it is to proclaim the Word.

I think I saw the same angels that took God's message of judgment to King Nebuchadnezzar in a vision:

> [13] In the visions I saw while lying in my bed, I looked, and there before me was a messenger, a holy one [angel], coming down from heaven.
>
> [14] He called in a loud voice: "Cut down the tree and trim off its branches; strip off its leaves and scatter its fruit. Let the animals flee from under it and the birds from its branches.
>
> [15] "But let the stump and its roots, bound with iron and bronze, remain in the ground, in the grass of the field. Let him be drenched with the dew of heaven, and let him live with the animals among the plants of the earth.
>
> [16] "Let his mind be changed from that of a man and let him be given the mind of an animal, till seven times pass by for him.
>
> [17] "The decision is announced by messengers, the holy ones [angels] declare the verdict, so that the

living may know that the Most High is sovereign over the kingdoms of men and gives them to anyone he wishes and sets over them the lowliest of men." (Daniel 4:13–17 NIV)

MINISTERING ANGELS

Listen, friends, I have had angels talk to me—instructing me, comforting me, strengthening me, blessing me—many times.

- 📖 If God could use an angel to strengthen Daniel during prayer (see Daniel 9:21), He can use an angel to help us today.
- 📖 If God could send an angel to reveal to Zechariah the meaning of a vision He was showing the prophet (see Zechariah 1:9), He can use an angel to communicate to us.
- 📖 If God could send the angel Gabriel to reveal the future to Daniel (see Daniel 8:16), He can use an angel to explain ideas to us.
- 📖 If God could use an angel to instruct Philip the evangelist what to do next (see Acts 8:26), He can use

an angel to give us directions.

📖 If God could use an angel to quicken Daniel's mind and give him the skill to understand the things of God (see Daniel 9:22), He can use an angel to give us insight and to help us understand His Word.

📖 If God could give the entire book of Revelation to John by an angel (see Revelation 1:1), He can use an angel to tell us about our future.

📖 If God could use an angel to explain a vision to Daniel (see Daniel 8:16), He can use an angel to clarify things for us.

One of these warrior angels I saw reminded me of the story in Joshua 5:13–15. One day near the city of Jericho, Joshua spotted a mighty warrior standing with his sword drawn. Joshua approached him and asked, "Are you for us or for our adversaries?"

"Neither," said this mighty being. "I have come as the commander of the army of the Lord."

Joshua quickly paid homage to the captain of the Lord's hosts and asked,

"What instructions from the Lord do you have for me?" The warrior angel gave him the divine plan for taking the city of Jericho.

I tell you, friends, God's angelic generals and lieutenants know how to do battle for the Lord.

> [17] The chariots of God are twenty thousand, even thousands of angels: the Lord is among them, as in Sinai, in the holy place.
>
> [Psalm 68:17]

Be sure, always, that you are on the Lord's side. His angels will watch over you and come to your rescue when you need that something extra.

Chapter 12

The Final War in the Cosmos

I heard a cry so desperate that it filled my heart with despair. "No hope, no hope!" the voice called. The mournful, hopeless cry came from a coffin. It was an endless wail of regret. "Oh, how awful!" I said.

"Come," said Jesus, "let's go closer." With that, He walked up to the coffin and looked inside. I followed and also peered in. It seemed that the evil spirits could not see us.

A dirty-gray mist filled the inside of the coffin. It was the soul of a man. As I watched, demons pushed their spears into the soul of the man in the coffin.

I will never forget the suffering of this soul. I cried to Jesus, "Let him out, Lord; let him out." The torment of his soul was such a terrible sight. If only he could get free! I pulled at Jesus' hand and begged Him to let the man out of his coffin.

WHY SOULS ARE LOST

Jesus said, "My child, peace, be still. This man was a preacher of the Word of God. There was a time when he served Me with all his heart and led many people to salvation. Many of his converts are still serving Me today.

"But the lust of the flesh and the deceitfulness of riches led him astray. He let Satan gain power over him. He had a big church, a fine car, a large income. He began to steal from the church offerings. He began to teach lies. Most of what he spoke was full of half-lies and half-truths.

"He would not let Me correct him. I sent My messengers to him to tell him to repent and preach the truth, but he loved the pleasures of this life more than the life of God. He knew not to teach or preach any other doctrine except the truth as revealed in the Bible.

"But before he died, he said that the Holy Spirit baptism was a lie and that those who claimed to have the Holy Spirit were hypocrites. He said you could be a drunkard and get to heaven, even without repentance.

"He said that God would not send anyone to hell—that God was too good to do that. He caused many good people to fall from the grace of the Lord. He even said that he did not need Me, for he was like a god. He went so far as to hold seminars to teach this false doctrine. He trampled My Holy Word under his feet. Yet, I continued to love him.

"My child, it is better to have never known Me than to know Me and turn back from serving Me," said the Lord.

"If only he had listened to You, Lord!" I cried. "If only he had cared about his soul and the souls of others."

"He would not listen to Me. When I called, he would not hear Me. He loved the easy life. I called and called him to repentance, but he would not come back to Me.

"One day he was killed and came immediately to this place in hell. Now Satan torments him for having once preached My Word and saved souls for My kingdom. This is his torment."

I watched the demons as they continued to march around and around the coffin. The man's heart beat, and real blood spurted from it. I will never forget his cries of pain and sorrow.

As we left, I saw another group of demons coming up to the coffin. They were about three feet tall, dressed in black clothes, with black hoods over their faces. They were taking shifts tormenting this soul.

THE DANGER OF PRIDE

I thought about how pride in all of us at times makes us unwilling to admit mistakes and ask for forgiveness. We refuse to repent and humble ourselves, and we go on as if we alone were forever right.

Listen, friend; hell is real, and demons are real! Please do not give in to evil spirits. Please do not go to hell.

Then God showed me a giant clock, stretching out across the whole world. I heard it ticking. The hour hand was nearing the twelve o'clock position, and the minute hand raced around until it stopped at three minutes before twelve. Stealthily, the minute hand moved toward the hour. As it moved, the ticking became louder and louder until it seemed to fill the whole earth.

The Lord spoke, and His voice sounded like a trumpet: "Listen and hear what My Spirit is saying to you. Be ready, for at a time you do not expect, I will come again. I hear the clock striking. It is twelve o'clock. The Bridegroom has come for His bride."

Then I realized that He had turned from showing me the horrors of hell to revealing the future and some of the events about the Second Coming. With conflicting feelings, I realized that the time for that glorious event is almost here.

Anticipating the Lord's coming, I echoed the words John shouted on Patmos, *"Even so, come, Lord Jesus"* (Revelation 22:20).

At the same time, I could not help but think of unsaved loved ones and of the violent, wrenching spiritual warfare that is being waged by God's people with Satan and his demons and evil spirits.

"What will become of this struggle?" I asked the Lord.

"Come with Me," Jesus said. And He took me to a very high place. "Behold!" was the single word of command that He spoke to me, and suddenly I was alone.

I looked toward space, and developing before my eyes was a scene I can hardly describe. Far away I could see Jesus coming in power and glory!

As He got nearer, I could tell that He was riding on a massive white horse. He looked like a triumphant conqueror.

Accompanying our Lord were armies of saints and angels. Every single saint and angel was dressed in a white robe.

[14] Now Enoch...prophesied about these men also, saying, "Behold, the Lord comes with ten thousands of His saints,

[15] "to execute judgment on all, to convict all who are ungodly among them of all their ungodly deeds

which they have committed in an ungodly way, and of all the harsh things which ungodly sinners have spoken against Him."

(Jude 1:14–15 NKJV)

WHEN THE CHURCH COMES BACK

A voice spoke to me, "This is the church returning with the Lord when He appears in glory. Armies of angel, hosts of angels, multiplied millions of angels will return with the Lord.

Another amazing thing I saw was that this army that accompanied Jesus had no weapons. They wore no armor and carried no shield. But each of them used *"the sword of the Spirit, which is the word of God"* (Ephesians 6:17).

As they neared the earth, I heard Jesus proclaim, "Behold, My bride!" And I understood what the Bible means when the church is called the bride of Christ.

Suddenly, my eyes were drawn to the earth, and before me was a large section of the countryside where the terrain was fairly level. I saw a scene that was almost unbelievable. Multiplied millions of soldiers were coming from every direction.

Foot soldiers, tanks, armored personnel carriers—people of every nationality prepared for war. Jets and bombers screamed through the air. These were modern, well-equipped armies.

What is this? I wondered. And the answer seemed to burn itself into my mind: *These armies are gathering for Armageddon!*

> [14] The armies of heaven were following him, riding on white horses and dressed in fine linen, white and clean.
>
> [15] Out of his mouth comes a sharp sword with which to strike down the nations. "He will rule them with an iron scepter." He treads the winepress of the fury of the wrath of God Almighty.
>
> [16] On his robe and on his thigh he has this name written: KING OF KINGS AND LORD OF LORDS.
>
> [17] And I saw an angel standing in the sun, who cried in a loud voice to all the birds flying in midair, "Come, gather together for the great supper of God,
>
> [18] so that you may eat the flesh of kings, generals, and mighty men, of horses and their riders, and the

flesh of all people, free and slave, small and great."

¹⁹ Then I saw the beast and the kings of the earth and their armies gathered together to make war against the rider on the horse and his army.

²⁰ But the beast was captured, and with him the false prophet who had performed the miraculous signs on his behalf. With these signs he had deluded those who had received the mark of the beast and worshiped his image. The two of them were thrown alive into the fiery lake of burning sulfur.

²¹ The rest of them were killed with the sword that came out of the mouth of the rider on the horse, and all the birds gorged themselves on their flesh.

(Revelation 19:14–21 NIV)

ARMAGGEDON AND BEYOND

Jesus and His army made a complete circuit of the whole world, and every person on earth saw Him. When the entourage arrived at Armageddon, 200 million soldiers had gathered from every nation to do battle with the Lord.

¹³ They have one purpose and will give their power and authority to the beast.

¹⁴ They will make war against the Lamb, but the Lamb will overcome them because he is Lord of lords and King of kings—and with him will be his called, chosen and faithful followers.

(Revelation 17:13–14 NIV)

Incredibly, when Jesus revealed Himself to the whole world, the leaders of the world's nations actually attempted to assault and attack the Lord. But it was no contest! Two hideous beings were first captured by the angels and thrown into the lake of fire.

"That is the Antichrist and the False Prophet," a voice told me.

Then—and I can hardly describe it!—Jesus, astride His massive, handsome, powerful white horse, began to speak.

As He spoke, it looked like laser beams shooting out of His mouth in the direction He faced. He turned around, and as He did, the armies began to fall.

Soldiers fell dead in their tracks. Jets tumbled out of the sky as their pilots died. The battlefield was a scene of utter chaos.

Without lifting a weapon, using only the words of His mouth, Jesus defeated all of the armies of the earth.

Then I saw a mighty warrior angel flying swiftly toward the battlefield that was littered with slain bodies and wrecked war machines. The warrior angel seized the devil and his angels and cast them into a huge abyss.

The angel used a large key that was hanging at his side to unlock the abyss and to lock it again when the devils and demons were safely sealed inside. (See Revelation 20:1–3.)

Later, I saw Satan and his hordes released for a short time, and they were still up to their old tricks. They again deceived some of the people of the earth and tried to lead a rebellion against God.

THE DEMISE OF SATAN AND HIS DEMONS

I was appalled to see these evil spirits persuade armies to march against God one more time. In a final apocalyptic scene, I saw fire come down from heaven and defeat all of Satan's army. Then, Jesus Himself cast Satan and his demons into the lake of fire for all eternity!

> [10] And the devil that deceived them was cast into the lake of fire and brimstone, where the beast and the false prophet are, and shall be tormented day and night for ever and ever.   (Revelation 20:10)

I saw the earth suddenly on fire! A great holocaust enveloped this entire planet, and I saw people standing before the judgment seat of God. Would the earth really burn up?

I wanted confirmation from the Word of God. Then He led me to Second Peter, where I learned that the universe will also be consumed by fire:

> [8] But do not forget this one thing, dear friends: With the Lord a day is like a thousand years, and a thousand years are like a day.
>
> [9] The Lord is not slow in keeping his promise, as some understand slowness. He is patient with you, not wanting anyone to perish, but everyone to come to repentance.

[10] But the day of the Lord will come like a thief. The heavens will disappear with a roar; the elements will be destroyed by fire, and the earth and everything in it will be laid bare.

[11] Since everything will be destroyed in this way, what kind of people ought you to be? You ought to live holy and godly lives

[12] as you look forward to the day of God and speed its coming. That day will bring about the destruction of the heavens by fire, and the elements will melt in the heat.

[13] But in keeping with his promise we are looking forward to a new heaven and a new earth, the home of righteousness.

(2 Peter 3: 8–13 NIV)

Oh, how the saints, the bride of Christ, the armies of the King rejoiced and praised God with the angels. Together, they worshipped the Lamb of God who is King of Kings and Lord of Lords.

REJOICE EVERMORE!

As God was giving me the final picture, I was swept up into the triumphant heavenly procession of redeemed saints as they paraded with the King of Kings and Lord of Lords. With gladness I realized that all of my hopes and dreams, as well as those of every believer, were finally and fully realized.

My friends, we will be free from Satan and every vestige of evil one day, if we remain true to God. You don't have to be manipulated by Satan and his demons. The power of Christ can set you free!

First, let me urge you to trust in Him as your Lord and Savior.

Second, know that Jesus will not live in the same heart with a demon. When the Lord comes in, the devils have to flee!

Third, learn what the Bible has to say about our spiritual enemies. Be aware of spiritual warfare. Stay eternally vigilant, and don't let your guard down against the devil.

Fourth, walk in victory every single day! Praise God, you can...*and with God's help, you will!*

Epilogue: A Final Appeal

All of us must be ready to meet the Lord. With all my heart, I urge you to be ready, *"for you know neither the day nor the hour in which the Son of Man is coming"* (Matthew 25:13 NKJV). Jesus Christ is coming back, and soon!

I want you to be ready. If you have never received Jesus Christ as your Lord and Savior, you can be saved, according to the Word of God:

> [16] For God so loved the world that He gave His only begotten Son, that whoever believes in Him should not perish but have everlasting life.
>
> (John 3:16 NKJV)

> [9] If you confess with your mouth the Lord Jesus and believe in your heart that God has raised Him

from the dead, you will be saved.

¹⁰ For with the heart one believes unto righteousness, and with the mouth confession is made unto salvation.

¹³ Whoever calls on the name of the LORD shall be saved.

(Romans 10:9–10, 13 NKJV)

Please pray this prayer right now:

Father, in the name of Jesus Christ, I come unto You, just as I am, a sinner. I have sinned against You and against heaven. I ask You, Lord Jesus, to forgive me and to come into my heart and save my soul. Let me be born again by the Spirit of the living God.

I give my life to You, Lord Jesus. I do believe that You are the Son of God. I give You thanks and praise and honor for redeeming me by Your precious blood. Amen.

If you have prayed this prayer with me and really believed what you prayed, you are now saved. You have asked Jesus Christ into your heart. Begin to confess Him with your lips and praise Him. To God be all praise and honor!

About the Author

Mary Kathryn Baxter was born in Chattanooga, Tennessee. She was brought up in the house of God. While she was still young, her mother taught her about Jesus Christ and His salvation.

Kathryn was born again at the age of nineteen. After serving the Lord for several years, she backslid for a season. The Spirit of the Lord would not release her, and she came back and gave her life anew to Christ. She still serves Him faithfully.

In the mid-1960s Kathryn moved with her family to Detroit, Michigan, where she lived for a time. She later moved to Belleville, Michigan, where she began to have visions from God.

In 1976, while she was living in Belleville, Jesus appeared to her in human form, in dreams, in visions, and in revelations. Since that time she has received many visitations from the Lord. During those visits He has shown her the depths, degrees, levels, and torments of lost souls in hell. She has also received many visions of heaven, the Great Tribulation, and the end of time.

During one period of her life, Jesus appeared to her each night for forty nights. He revealed to her the horrors of hell and the glories of heaven. He told her that this message is for the whole world.

Ministers, leaders, and saints of the Lord speak very highly of her and her ministry. The movement of the Holy Spirit is emphasized in all her services, and many miracles have occurred in them. The gifts of the Holy Spirit with demonstrations of power are manifested in her meetings as the Spirit of God leads and empowers her. She loves the Lord with all her heart, mind, soul, and strength and desires above all else to be a soulwinner for Jesus Christ.

She is truly a dedicated handmaiden of the Lord. Her calling is specifically in the area of dreams, visions, and revelations. She was ordained as a minister in 1983 at the Full Gospel Church of God in Taylor, Michigan. She now ministers with the National Church of God in Washington, D.C.